# TELL YOUR EATING DISORDER TO F*** OFF

Separating YOU from your eating disorder

## RECLAIM YOUR POWER

And manifest the life you desire
AND so desperately deserve

By KATE PURCELL

HEMBURY BOOKS

**HEMBURY**
—BOOKS—

Copyright © Kate Purcell 2026
First published by Hembury Books in 2026
hemburybooks.com.au
info@hemburybooks.com
Paperback ISBN 9781923517721
Ebook ISBN 9781923517684

The moral right of the author has been asserted.
All rights reserved. No portion of this book may be reproduced in any form without permission from the author and publisher, except as permitted by Australian copyright law.

 A catalogue record for this book is available from the National Library of Australia

This book is dedicated to my amazing partner in crime, Leon. You are my rock, and you support me in any way you can, even through all this ED stuff. You never, ever judge me, and I know you love me whatever size I am. You're incredible and I love that you are not only my partner but my best friend.

I would also like to dedicate this book to all of the men/women/boys/girls out there, battling with an eating disorder. You are so strong and resilient and picking up this book is indeed a sign that you are moving forward and telling your eating disorder to F**k Off! You've got this!

# CONTENTS

About the author — 6

Foreword — 7

Introduction — 9

### Chapter 1 - Finding YOU — 13
- YOU are NOT your eating disorder — 13
- Who are you? Exploring your identity — 15
- What are your personal values? — 18
- What are your life goals? — 20
- Aligning with your goals and personal values — 23

### Chapter 2 - Understanding your ED — 26
- The Characteristics of an eating disorder — 26

### Chapter 3 - Moving Forward — 41
- The Christmas Experiment — 41
- What matters, what doesn't. — 45
- Finding Courage, Hope & Resilience Within — 47
- Building Self-worth & Self-love — 52

### Chapter 4 - The final journey home — 64
- Back to basics – seeking help to help myself — 64
- Loosening its grip — 67
- Kate is back in the driver's seat — 69

## CHAPTER 5 - FINAL NOTES — 71
- Balance, not addiction, or obsession — 71
- A note for loved ones — 74

## CHAPTER 6 - MANIFESTATION WORKBOOK — 77
- Introduction to manifestation — 77
- Free writing exercise — 80
- See the life you want exercise — 82
- Setting intentions — 84
- Action steps — 86
- Life domains — 86
- Dream Job Visualisation — 88
- The Tree of Love Exercise — 89
- Self-love in practice — 91
- Self-Love Energy Suckers — 91
- Positive Self-Love — 91

## CONCLUSION — 97

## ACKNOWLEDGEMENTS — 100

# About the Author

Kate Purcell is an author, speaker, peer worker and lived-experience expert. For the first 26 years of her life, Kate lived through various mental disorders, including schizoaffective disorder and psychosis. First diagnosed with anorexia nervosa at the age of fourteen, she remains vigilant in her relationship with food and weight. Her work is motivated by her experiences and a desire to help others through their own trying times.

Now in her forties, Kate is happy, vibrant and healthy. She continually strives to give hope to others who have none. In her honest and raw second book, Tell *Your Eating Disorder* to F\*\*k *Off*, Kate gets into the trenches with her readers, joining them on their journey as she traverses her own. Her first book, *Hope Inc*, is a memoir of illness and recovery.

Both of Kate's books act as a supportive reminder that while the eating disorder journey never truly ends, the path does get smoother.

Kate lives in Perth WA with her partner, Leon, and their fur-baby, Pan. She loves music, fashion, seeing her friends and sitting in the sunshine at her local pub. Kate is a passionate soul and believes in the statement that 'Hope is passion for what is possible'.

# FOREWORD

I first stepped into the field of eating disorders almost by accident in 1991, when I was working in London in the United Kingdom. I had taken over the management of a private hospital's eating disorder unit at a time when cognitive behaviour therapy was becoming increasingly influential and widely applied in the treatment of eating disorders.

When I began in this role, I focused on two things.

First, a psychiatrist colleague and I decided to take ourselves out of the hospital and into the community. We attended support groups across London that were run by people with lived experience—people who had navigated and recovered from an eating disorder. We went there to listen. We spoke with facilitators and participants about what they believed was genuinely helpful, and what they felt was unhelpful, in their treatment experiences.

Second, inside the unit, I watched, listened, and asked the people I was working with to help me understand their world. Together, we explored the resistance they felt toward treatment, the drive to maintain certain behaviours, and the fear and uncertainty that came with letting those behaviours go.

Over time, this shaped the way I understood treatment. It became clear to me that it wasn't enough to rely solely on statistical significance from research, or even on clinical significance in terms of evidence-based practice. What mattered just as much—perhaps even more—was meaningful significance: what people with lived expertise and their families say about what is, was, and can be truly helpful in the treatment of eating

In 1996, after returning to Perth in Western Australia, three colleagues and I began exploring the idea of developing a dedicated child and adolescent eating disorder unit. Our aim was to bring together the three elements we believed were essential: robust research, strong clinical application, and a deep understanding of lived expertise—including the perspectives of families.

It wasn't long after this that I met Kate Purcell. Over the past 20 years, I've had the privilege of observing and walking alongside Kate—not just from a distance, but in a meaningful and sustained way. I've watched her navigate extraordinarily complex conditions, including anorexia and schizoaffective disorder. But more importantly, I've watched her achievements.

Her strength, her determination, and her commitment to helping others have been remarkable. That drive—her purpose—has culminated in her current work, Tell Your Eating Disorder to F Off, a powerful articulation of hope, agency, and lived wisdom.

Kate's new book is an essential read — whether you are a clinician, someone currently living with an eating disorder, or a family member wanting to understand and support a loved one. Kate has a rare and valuable gift: she combines her lived-experience with practical, evidence-based clinical strategies. Some of these techniques draw on cognitive behaviour therapy, others on acceptance and commitment therapy. She encourages readers to consider their personal values — and to reflect on how an eating disorder may have slowly pulled them away from living in alignment with those values.

Kate also recognises that for many people, an eating disorder can feel like a form of protection. And in the early stages, that protective shell may serve a perceived purpose. But over time, the very same pattern becomes imprisoning. It restricts life, limits possibilities, and distances people from the goals and the person they hoped to become.

With both sensitivity and honesty, Kate guides the reader through a journey of self-discovery — drawing from her own recovery. The result is a deeply human, courageous, and insightful roadmap for reclaiming life. - *Chris Harris December 2025*

# INTRODUCTION

> "Struggle is nature's way of strengthening it"
> Anon

There are several reasons why I am writing this book. Firstly, it is a message to those out there who struggle with an eating disorder, to take back the control of their very existence, and move away from the need to be so focused on weight/food/appearance. I want to give those people an excuse to really look right into the eyes and the soul of their eating disorder, and hopefully find some peace from it, and feel empowered, despite its presence. Another reason is to hopefully give the family, friends and loved ones of someone with an eating disorder, not only some understanding around what an eating disorder actually is, but also how it is experienced, and give them a good dose of hope that there is, in fact, a way through to the other side. The other reason is, in fact, my own efforts to tell *my* eating disorder to F*** off. I am 41 years old, and I can't keep count of how many days, months, and years my eating disorder has consumed me. To varying degrees. These days I am doing a lot better, and in the process of finally moving away from my eating disorder. I have discovered several truths and pearls of wisdom that continue to keep me well and happy. These truths and pearls of wisdom, I am wanting to share with you in this book, and hopefully this will help you move forward. I still have a slight way to go in my journey, and writing this book is part of me grabbing the bull by the horns and telling my ED to f**k off. I want the rest of my life to be the best of my life, and an ED does not have to be a part of this; in fact, it is imperative that I learn what is needed to live a life, not consumed by weight, food or appearance.

I'll tell you a little bit more about my journey in this chapter, and then I will be going through everything that I feel is necessary to start moving in a different direction. I have a wealth of knowledge to share with you, dear reader.

I suffered from low self-worth and low self-confidence from a young age. And I have always been critical of my appearance, even at the age of 8, I remember looking in the mirror and hating my bum and the fact that it stuck out. My relationship with my twin brother didn't help matters, as he was the complete opposite of me, very loud, outgoing, funny and confident. In comparison, I felt innately flawed and worthless because I was not like him.

Enter a bit of teasing in early high school, and rejection from a boy, the ED was beckoning. I remember going on a strict diet at the end of year 8, and so it began… Obsession with weight loss and food intake. By the time I got to the beginning of year 10, I was very underweight and after an assessment at Princess Margaret hospital, I was diagnosed with Anorexia Nervosa.

2 years of going further downhill, Anorexia literally consumed every ounce of my being. Many traumatic hospitalisations, many tube feeds, and complete isolation from family and friends (physical and emotional). I was miserable, and I was powerless to stop my ED from taking over. After an incident where I ran away from hospital and pulled my feeding tube out on the side of the road, my parents decided to take charge and send me to a private psychiatric clinic, which I did not feel ready for, in any way, shape or form. But I literally had no choice but to start looking directly into the eyes and soul of my ED. It took several months before I started to tackle things, but eventually I did. I started to gain weight and eat normal foods at normal times. The nurses and other patients began to heal me, and then, when I felt a bit more ready, I began to heal myself. After a 7 month stay, the clinic felt like my second home. But a spark was alight. It was Kate's spirit that sparked up, and I started to rediscover who I was, perhaps for the first time.

It was an epic process of self-exploration, and whilst the journey was one of the hardest things I have ever been through, I started to get a thirst for life again, and a sense of empowerment. Food and weight were simply not as important as they used to be. Life was beckoning... and happiness not so elusive.

This is not the end of my journey by any means, though. I was no longer in the very depths of my ED after my 7-month stay at the clinic (I was well into my recovery, which more than anything else, was very exciting and liberating), but weight, food and appearance again became an obsession again much later down the track. I still had further lessons to learn about myself and my world.

Fast forward 25 years, and I am still grappling with ED. Grappling with an obsession around food and weight. I will fill you in a little bit about the goings-on of that time in between (and if you have read my first book you would have a good idea already). After equally unpleasant experiences with mental ill-health, things eventually came to a head when I became psychotic at the age of 25. Fast-forward a year or so and I was then diagnosed with schizoaffective disorder and promptly medicated with anti-psychotic medication. Enter: Weight gain (very common with anti-psychotics). This was traumatic for me, as I had always been small. I grappled with this for years but came to a point where I didn't care so much. My life was grand. I had an amazing partner, an amazing job and amazing friends. The weight/food thing just didn't matter so much anymore. But I did gain a fair bit of weight, to the point where I started to look at weight loss again. I lost a fair amount of weight with Jenny Craig, so I was reasonably content. But keeping the weight off was a struggle. My obsession with it ebbed and flowed, at times it consumed me more than other times. And then, about 2 years ago, I set a goal to lose a little bit of weight; eat healthy, went to the gym etc. I did manage to lose a fair bit, and I have managed to maintain at a healthy weight. What I didn't expect to have happen, though, is that I started to become obsessed with the weight loss, and I thought about appearance and food way too much. The ED grabbed hold of me once again, and even though I am not excessively underweight, the ED was controlling, obsessive and mean. This is why I will touch on the fact later in this book that ED's can, of course, occur at any weight or size, not just when someone is very underweight.

But I had a huge realisation that the ED was rearing its ugly head, and it was not only making me obsessed, but it was also turning me into someone that I didn't like, very judgmental, impatient and highly strung. I was completely unaware of this, and I got the wake-up call that I needed. I am on a better path now, back to feeling like myself, much more grateful for the life I am living, and very much working to overcome this addiction and obsession with weight. Hence back to what I was saying around my reasons for writing this book. This is not only for you, dear readers, or family and friends; this is for me. It is about self-exploration and acceptance that we must work through the intricate inner workings of our ED's. As I said, I want the rest of my life to be the best of my life, and I am determined to not have an ED be a part of that. This is what we all deserve. I have learnt incredible amounts of knowledge and many pearls of wisdom when it comes to ED's. I have the keys that are needed, I just need to remember them and where to find them, to help me, and then help you.

I am reclaiming my power by doing this, and I am going to swiftly tell my ED to F**k off. Let me help you do the same, because we all deserve a life free from its shackles and soul-destroying ways.

Ready. Set. Go

# Chapter 1
## Finding You

### • YOU are NOT your eating disorder

> "I hate everything about you, so why, do I still love you?"
> Three Days Grace

This song lyric pretty much sums it up, as you will see in a sec. In short: *you are not your eating disorder*; it is only a very small part of you, which simply got *louder* and bigger, the more you fed it with obsessive, compulsive and negative eating disordered thoughts and behaviours. The *louder* it became, well, to be put simply... *you* started to disappear. This is one of the first things you must recognise and accept, at the beginning of your journey to the other side. It is incredibly easy to forget that there is a beautiful, unique, deserving soul under the surface, but it has been muted, the bigger and more prominent, your eating disorder became. After I (many moons ago) realized that this eating disorder part of me, was *not* me, I started the huge process of actually exploring who I was, completely separate from my ED. I started to see it for what it was. And I *hated* it. When you break it down, your ED is not a good part of you.... It is judgmental, critical, and mean. It is obsessive, compulsive and perfectionistic to the n'th degree. And it's making you unhappy, and sick. Yet (somehow) we love it. We love the control it has over us because it feels safe and familiar, and we somehow love its somewhat comforting shackles.

We might ask ourselves the question, "Where do I end, and my eating disorder begin?" The answer to this question does not have to be so elusive. It is straightforward. Going through an eating disorder I feel is terribly confusing and disempowering, because we forget who we are. As previously mentioned, it can take over completely (or just a bit, like in my current situation). The eating disorder begins taking over your soul and spirit, either entirely or partially. Therefore, the question of where you end, and the eating disorder begins, is simple. You, your spirit, is still there, but it is muffled and dampened. You are there at the same time, in the same space as your ED (which is only your shell), and every time you smile or laugh, there is a sparkle of your spirit that shines through. And if you can become aware of this happening, you will be halfway there. You will remember that 'oh, there is still a sparkle that can't be taken away entirely'. When you feed *your* soul with negative eating disordered thoughts and eating disordered behaviours, you are in turn feeding its soul. And it will get stronger and louder. In turn, when you feed *your* soul with positive, healthy, empowering thoughts and behaviours, *your* unique, beautiful, deserving spirit gets the limelight for a second and all of a sudden, we remember who we are. We must hold onto this, and come to see the difference between *your* wonderful, sparkly soul, and the eating disorders unhappy, obsessive and controlling soul. What I hope happens with yourself, dear reader, is that you start to become more familiarised with this unique, beautiful soul that you have, and start exploring what is actually important, and what is not. Your eating disorder will more than likely tell you that being disciplined and/or thin is what is important, but I'm hedging a bet that *you* see things differently. A question I like to ask myself from time to time, when I am in battle with my ED, is, what will I treasure the most when I am at the end of my life, and looking back? The answer to this, for me, is memories, love, relationships, adventure, family and friends. Everything that gets taken away when your ED is wreaking havoc on your world. It is simply ridiculous to think that we might look back and say to ourselves, "I value and/or treasure the fact that I was thin". Remember that.

## • Who are you? Exploring your identity

If you believe that your ED is part of your identity, I am going to have to let you know at this point that this is incorrect. Your ED may lead you to believe that your ED = you. I will tell you this, though. At one point in time, when my parents expressed to me that they were going to send me to the private psychiatric clinic to help me, this was met with an intense amount of negativity, anger and shock. I, regrettably, physically pushed and shoved both of my parents in an effort to regain control over the situation. Does that sound like something you would do in your right mind? No. Your ED mutes and muffles your true spirit and creates more of a shell over and around you.... and this shell is terrified of losing control. It was this terror that pushed me to the point where I was physically violent. It is imperative that you begin to separate your ED from who *you* are. Remember that your ED is simply a shell, and your unique spirit (who *you* are) is right in the centre... but completely powerless and stomped upon. Part of taking the reins back is simply remembering this truth.

So, when it comes to rediscovering (or discovering for the first time even) your true self and your true identity, I am going to put this to you. Let this question of "who am I?" excite you. Once you know who *you* are, what qualities you naturally portray, what your likes and dislikes are, and what is important to *you*, you can start to build your new life around these answers. The life that you are currently living, if you are letting your ED take over (even just a little bit), is likely not to be the sort of life that makes you feel happy, healthy or empowered. It is likely you feel scared, controlled and disempowered (even though we think *we* are in control, it is actually the ED that is controlling our very essence and every single decision we make, every day).

When I was in the midst of going through the beginning stages of my recovery, and in the psychiatric clinic, I eventually started to explore my identity. A part of this was realising I was not alone, I had other patients and nurses working with me on this, because I was building helpful and positive friendships and kinships during my time there. Seeing myself through their kind eyes was definitely helpful, and what I was experiencing with them was nourishing and nurturing. I began to remember…" I am loving and kind" … and "I am worthy". This eventually led to … "I am deserving of good things". Prior to this my ED took all that away from me. It told me that I was *not* deserving or worthy, it told me I was *selfish* and bad. If this is your current experience, remember that *you are not at all*, selfish or bad… this is simply your ED wreaking havoc, and it is literally tricking us to believe these things that are simply not true. Once I started with this huge change of perspective, I had fun with it. At the time of my recovery at the clinic, I went to a piercing shop with another patient, who became a friend, and I got my tongue pierced! And I started to be a bit of a rebel (smoking cigarettes - which I wouldn't recommend). But this was all about me finding myself… probably for the first time ever, at age 16. I started to buy clothes that I liked, and I started to love music again (that was a huge one). I was taking the reins back, and I wanted to have fun. And I knew (most of the time) that I was deserving of this. When you start to come into yourself and when you start celebrating you, this puts the ED right back where it belongs.… itself – *muted and lost for words.* Your own inner power can silence the ED once and for all (this happens slowly at first). Once this started happening, I started to set goals and allowed myself to dream of things that I was wanting to experience in my life. I remember writing down things like, going out for dinner with my family, going on a fun holiday to the Gold Coast, or going to a music festival. My thirst for life was peaking, and whenever my ED was trying to tell me all the negatives and whenever it was trying really hard to grab a hold of me, these dreams kept me much stronger and more motivated.

Look, in the process of finding yourself again, your ED will ark up. It is inevitable. But now you know the difference between who *you* are and what your eating disorder is. It will more than likely be a battle, especially if you are in the beginning stages of recovery... but it will get easier. I promise you, dear reader. You will get stronger, and your ED will eventually get weaker. So, what I want you to do now is not only try to identify some of your positive qualities but also identify some positive goals (and dreams) for your future... really dig deep and find within yourself that sense of motivation and even excitement.

I AM:

___

___

___

___

5 SHORT TERM GOALS/PLANS:

___

___

___

___

___

5 LONG TERM GOALS/PLANS:

___

___

___

___

___

I will say one additional thing about self-exploration and finding out more about yourself. It is great to know what you like and dislike in general terms, but there was one other thing that I had to explore around this. And that was food. We would be kidding ourselves to say that food has not been as much of an issue as weight and appearance. Food is probably something that you have been rather afraid of, and/or obsessive about. What you need to do aswell in your recovery is build a better, healthier relationship with food. When you are getting the help you need regarding weight etc, it is important to remember, in the recovery equation, that food must be looked at and explored. When I was in recovery, it took me quite a long time to get rid of the fear around food, especially "normal" foods. I needed a lot of support, particularly in the beginning. But once I started to actually *enjoy* food again, another thing that ended up being really fun, was to explore my likes and dislikes around food. I started to experiment with different foods and push my comfort zone (for instance, mars lite bars I remember was my first new experience with chocolate). If this is still a fair way off in your ED journey, that's ok. But eventually you will get to this stage, and all I can say is *enjoy* it. We all deserve to enjoy food, and we all deserve to be nourished by food, so exploring your relationship with it is without a doubt, a very important part of recovery and reclaiming your power.

I will end this chapter by saying, just do everything you can to identify and/or remember who you truly are. If listening to a certain song excites you, then listen to it and feel empowered in this experience. If being creative lights you up, then do this as much as you can. Your beautiful soul will definitely thank you for your efforts simply in discovering and affirming who *you* are, separate from your ED.

## • What are your personal values?

"Personal values are deeply held beliefs and principles that guide individuals in their thoughts, actions and decision making. They reflect what is important to a person and shape their identity and behaviour. Personal values are often influenced by factors such as culture, family, religion, mentors, and personal experiences."

I am going to bite the bullet and say, that what your ED values and what you value are probably very, very different. Recognising this is important. We will explore a little more in a later chapter, what is actually important, and what isn't. But this values work, starts right here.

As an ex-alcohol and drug counsellor, I worked with clients' personal values very regularly. In AOD counselling, it important for the client to recognise that their alcohol and/or drug use often doesn't allow them to be the kind of person they want to be. They are, more often than not, misaligning their decisions and actions with their inherent values. This creates an inner conflict, which in turn affects their moods, their general wellbeing and their self-esteem and/or self-worth. I am going to say, quite bluntly, that it works the same when an ED is ruling (or somewhat ruling) your life. I actually see ED's as being very similar to an addiction – an addiction to weight loss or an addiction to thinking/obsessing about food, weight and appearance. When your ED is calling the shots so to speak, I highly doubt that you are (in terms of your behaviour and decisions) living in alignment with your most important values.

For instance, being caring and kind might be very important to you. But your ED might end up alienating your friends and family. You may, deep down, value loyalty. Emphasizing unwavering trust, commitment and support with family and friends, but again, when ED is wreaking havoc in your world, you may not be living in alignment with this value. This is when the ED may actually turn this around further and tell you are selfish and bad, and certainly not worthy or deserving of good things. Your self-esteem and self-worth could potentially hit a huge low, because of this. The fact that you are not living in alignment with your values and the fact that your ED capitalises on this inner conflict, and makes you even weaker and more controllable, will continue to keep you trapped and powerless.

So, what I would like you to do now, dear reader, is dig deep, to identify what values are truly important to you in life and then reflect on how your ED affects your ability to align with these important values. Recognise, overarching all of this, just how this (probable) misalignment is affecting your self-esteem, self-worth and general emotional/mental well-being. Allow yourself to daydream, ever so slightly, about just how you would feel if you were able to completely align with what is important to *you*.

## • What are your life goals?

When you were little, I bet you dreamt of what you wanted your life to be when you "grew up". I remember when I was a little girl, I wanted to be a bride. I also remember that I dreamt of being happy. When I think about that little girl, and what has happened to those goals and dreams, I feel sad...for the time spent consumed by an ED. That little girl deserves to have her dreams come true, and that little girl deserves to be happy. When an ED is taking over your life, these goals and dreams tend to go by the wayside. Because when an ED is part of your world, the most important thing becomes being thin. Chances are, you have lost your connection to that little girl, and you've totally confused your priorities... and lost your way.

Have a think about this. This may make you feel sad. Now that you have come to this realisation though, you will hopefully regain a strong desire to reconnect with your younger self. This is possible, all you need, moving forward is that intention to reconnect with her and start thinking about what she (*you*) wants for her future. Of course, sometimes our goals and dreams change as we get older, so what you wanted when you were a little girl, may be different to now. But I am betting not only have you lost this connection to your younger self, but you have also lost touch with yourself *now*... and what your goals and dreams are in this present day. So, I want you firstly, to start exploring this inside. What do I want my future to look like? And do I want my ED to be a part of my future? How will remaining a slave to my ED affect how my life plays out? And when you're answering these questions, remember that little girl, that *deserving* little girl. Do you want to fall madly in love and get married one day?

Do you want a family of your own? What sort of career do you want? What are your passions in life and how can you build a life around this answer? If your ED has a tight grip on you and your mindset, it will probably be telling you that you are *not* deserving of any of these good things, but this is how it tricks you. There is no truth in its words…I want you to completely separate the words that your ED speaks (that happiness will never be on the cards for you…you don't deserve it), and what *you* want in your future… because it is like comparing night and day.

Once you can acknowledge that you deserve all the happiness in the world, just like anyone else; you can start dreaming and planning. This may take a long time to materialize if you're still in the grips of your ED, but I 100% still encourage you to do this dreaming and planning. This is where recovery begins, with a thought that 'Hey, I want more than this'…'I want to win this battle'… 'I want to be happy'… 'This is what I want'…

These dreams and plans are going to further ignite your unique spirit and make you stronger. This is *you*, feeding *yourself* healthy and positive thoughts, and therefore pushing the ED out of the way, and putting it on mute… even for a mere moment.

Once you get a clearer picture of what it is that you want in your life, and what you want your life to be, I want you to remind yourself of this daily. Even multiple times throughout the day. There is going to be a battle with your ED, but you will win, by starting with these small steps forward. Allow yourself to just daydream. This feeds *your* soul what it needs most. Positivity.

I remember from when I was consumed by my ED, when I was a teenager, I could not even conceive of my life being any different. I understand that might be where you are right now, dear reader. I am still confident though, that by reading this book and acknowledging that your ED is indeed separate from who *you* really are… that a small seed will be planted, and even if all you can muster right now, is a 5-minute daydream about your life being different, better, happier… this is enough. This can grow over time.

Eventually, this 5-minute daydream can turn into an hour daydream and can then turn into actual plans – goals – short-term and long-term. For me, I remember a few things that I put into place quite quickly. I booked tickets for adventure world, I started karate classes, and then planned a trip to the gold coast for the following year... I was still in the beginning stages of recovery, but this planning and goal setting was only a good thing for me at the time. Further down the track in recovery, I started working at a kindy centre (1 day a week) and at Wendys on a casual basis. This allowed me to earn an income and buy things for myself that I wanted.

I will tell you another thing that helped me move forward in my recovery, when I started to remember who I was and how much power I actually had in my own life... I started to make dreams and plans with other people in my life... at the time, for myself, it was other patients at the clinic – some other patients experiencing an ED, but not necessarily - I was befriending a select few other kind patients too. And we would talk about things that we wanted for our future. And this made us all accountable. It also built anticipation and excitement (which is like kryptonite to an ED).

Momentum will keep building, and once things begin to move forward, it will get easier (and more enjoyable!!). So just keep dreaming and planning, you beautiful souls.

I will encourage you now, to pen down a few short-term and a few long-term goals....

**SHORT TERM GOALS:**
___
___
___

**LONG TERM GOALS:**
___
___
___

## *Aligning with your goals and personal values*

Aligning with your goals and values requires a reflection on one thing: The decisions you make, the thoughts you think, the actions you take, either move you towards where you wish to be, and towards who you want to be, or they move you away from where you wish to be, and away from who you want to be; and how you show up in your one precious life, on a daily basis. This is why it is so important to clarify your true goals and values, because if you can't recognise them, and be aware of them, you may continue to flounder and live a life that is not ideal for you. You will continue to feel lost and unfulfilled. When you can articulate exactly what you want to move towards, and when you start making decisions based on this knowledge, you will feel better about life, better about yourself and have very little inner conflict. I often used to say to my clients that their alcohol and/or drug use will continue to make them feel bad about themselves, because they are not living in alignment with what is important to them. The same goes for eating disorders. As we have already mentioned, that eating disordered part of you, is not nice. It is obsessive, controlling and mean. And what your eating disorder does on a daily basis, is turn you into someone that you don't want to be. It continues to influence the decisions you make, the thoughts you think, and the actions you take; and when you really explore who you are, which we will do much more of throughout this book; you will hopefully realise and come to the conclusion that the way you are living your life currently, will never make you happy, because of this gross misalignment between what you do, who you are, and your current decisions, thoughts and actions. This realisation may be difficult to swallow, and it may make you sad that you have been living this kind of life for so long. However, it should also create more of an intrinsic motivation to do things differently. You will very much need this motivation in the battle that is before you with your ED. Your ED will keep telling you what is important, but now that you have acknowledged the sort of life and self that you truly want, you can fight back.

These realisations will, in turn, give *you* more power over your ED. Because you are truly able to separate the ED part of you, and the *true you*...the one that has been muffled and dampened, the one whose voice has been unfortunately lost and drowned out completely.

So, again, I ask you, dear reader, to really dig deep, explore and daydream about what you want your life to be, and more importantly, what you don't want your life to be. I am betting that the kind of life you want, and the kind of person you want to be, does not include an ED and its controlling, soul-destroying ways. Like I said previously, the more you can explore and familiarise yourself with the real *you*, the better your chances of beating this thing. Think of your goals and values as an internal compass, directing you towards a life that will make you happy and more peaceful. Say you have a goal of falling in love and getting married... do everything you can to prepare for this. Get healthy in body and mind, work on yourself, and try and foster positive relationships with the people already in your life. This is not an easy feat, and it might seem like a long way away, but if you can make decisions every day, that move you towards fulfilling that dream, think the healthy, positive thoughts and take positive action (even in a small way), the more you will be aligning with this goal, the better you will feel, and once repeated many times, you will eventually be able to acknowledge that you, dear reader, are taking the reins back... and the easier it will become to move away from your eating disorder and towards a life that you love. Remember: You deserve to be happy, and you deserve to have a life that reflects your deepest hopes and desires.

What I would like you to do now, is reflect on how you can move towards your happy, fulfilled life, in even the smallest way...today. Show up today and do something that gives *you* the power back. Whether that is allowing yourself to laugh out loud, watching a funny movie (sparks your real, authentic self), or whether that is by jotting down your goals, dreams and values and daydreaming about a better life for 10 minutes.

So, what is this one step going to look like today?

**TODAY, I WILL TAKE ACTION TOWARDS A BETTER LIFE BY:**

_____
_____
_____
_____
_____

Now that you have discovered who you truly are, what is important to you, and what you want your life to be...you are halfway there. When an eating disorder rules your world, we simply forget all this, because it literally consumes you. If there is one message that I want you to take from this chapter, it is that you are deserving of living a life that you love. So, when you daydream about the life that you want for yourself – familiarise yourself with this more and more - I want you to solidly remind yourself that not only is this possible, but also that you are 100% deserving of this. Always remember that deserving little girl and always remember your beautiful sparkle.

# CHAPTER 2
## UNDERSTANDING YOUR ED

### The Characteristics of an eating disorder

Characteristics are defined as "typical of a particular person, place, or thing". In this case, with eating disorders, what are the typical traits, qualities or experiences? If you, dear reader, are struggling with an eating disorder, you will most likely be able to answer this question with ease. It is still helpful, however, to articulate and acknowledge these typical characteristics, because it may help further motivate us for positive change.

When I think of the term eating disorder. I get many words coming to the forefront of my mind. One of the most potent words that comes to mind is controlling. Or to use different language, the ability to maintain influence or authority over. Every ounce of your eating disorder is controlling; your eating disorder has authority over your thoughts, actions and behaviour, on daily basis. Think about this. You are not in the driver's seat, of your own life. The ED is in the driver's seat. When it comes to what *you* think, what *you* feel and what *you* do... the ED is influencing all of these factors. And it is terrified of *your power*; it is terrified of losing the control. That is why it is constantly dictating to you, how to live your life; it is dictating what your priorities are, and it is telling you what is important (to it). If it is consistently dictating the terms, you will stay under its tight grasp, and it will continue to hold the power and control. This, again, is why it is so crucial to separate yourself from the ED completely. See it for what it is. A part of you (the shell) that in itself is an entity, (a thing with a distinct and independent existence). It is independent from you (free from outside control; not subject to another's authority). The ED will keep feeding you thoughts and feelings that, in essence, keep you trapped and controlled. The ED will keep feeding you what its priorities are and keep telling you what is important. In the beginning stages of the development of your ED, it may have been your experience feeling that you *were* completely in control. If you were suffering with low self-esteem, you may have used body weight and food intake as a means of gaining control and self-worth. However, the ED quickly takes over, when you are highly vulnerable and impressionable. All of a sudden, your sense of control simply disappears, when your ED starts taking hold and running the show. You mistakenly see the control, as yours, but you are actually completely powerless. This was 100% my experience. I felt trapped by the ED, I felt frightened because I didn't know how to get back the control and actually move forward toward a happier, healthier life. Like I said, the ED is terrified of losing control, and when you start to get *your power* back, it will ark up. But the more you familiarise yourself with your unique, healthy, rational self, and the more you start feeding yourself positive thoughts and taking positive action, the weaker your ED will become. You must be persistent though, because your ED certainly will be. It is a battle, but if you do the work, you can defeat your ED once and for all. Take the control back now, remember, the ED is the enemy, not your ally by any means (however, we do delve further into this concept later).

    Another word that comes to mind when I think of what an eating disorder is, is obsession. No doubt, your ED has you obsessing over many things (of which aren't that important). Your weight, different aspects of your appearance, your calorie intake, your levels of exercise. I know for myself, the obsessiveness got to the point of severe obsessive-compulsive behaviours, in relation to weighing and measuring foods and liquids, weighing myself multiple times a day, everything being on a strict schedule, knowing exactly what I would be doing at any given time throughout any given day. This is obsessiveness at a critical level, but that was my life for a period of time, when an eating disorder ruled absolutely every part of my existence, including what I was doing at each minute, of each day. I was miserable. I remember sitting with my old case manager at Princess Margaret Hospital; she was a psychologist. I sat there and relayed to her the fact that every moment, of every day, I could tell her exactly what I would be doing. I was in tears. My life (outside of hospital – between admissions) was 100% controlled by my eating disorder. The obsession with weight, time, food etc, actually terrified me. I didn't know who I was anymore, I felt like I was just a shell, there was no Kate left. No more of Kate's unique sparkle, I was consumed.

Whilst this particular type of obsessive behaviour may not be something you can relate to, or maybe it is… the one thing I intrinsically know that you will relate to, is the overarching obsession with your weight. This is at the very crux of eating disorders. If we didn't care about our weight, our eating disorder would lose its power. It is the obsessive search and drive for weight loss, that drives our behaviours and our actions, every day – not to mention our thoughts. And I still, to this day, can understand this drive. On any given day, when I step on the scales in the morning, I am setting myself up for potential pain, depending on the number that stares back at me. I have had days where I was completely consumed by that number, it made what would have been a wonderful day, an absolute nightmare. The thoughts came…. "You are fat", "You're not thin enough". And talk about obsessive?! Whilst for people who are lucky enough to not be affected by an eating disorder, it may cause them to curse for a mere moment, but it would be left at that. They would indeed, go about their day as they normally would. For people that have that controlling, nasty entity taking up space in their soul, and experience of life, this number actually has the power to take them over completely, Because of the sheer obsessiveness that begins with seeing that number on the scales.

## TELL YOUR EATING DISORDER TO F*** OFF

And what about 'perfectionism' as a characteristic? I have heard, over the years, that a lot of people who develop an eating disorder have a perfectionistic streak, and to be honest, I couldn't initially relate to this as I for one was not a high achiever at school, I literally didn't really even care about my grades. All that mattered to me was becoming thin and definitely in the beginning, being accepted and liked by others. I needed validation that I was ok... and enough. Having said that, nowadays I see the perfectionistic streak in me, but this still relates to the same themes. Weight and other people's approval. With these things, I am absolutely perfectionistic, because I must weigh a certain number, or I feel like shit. Anything more than that will just not do. If 1 person out of 20 dislikes me, that is just not good enough. I have done some work around this, but it is still something I need help with. I feel that perfectionistic streaks, can never really work for anyone. There is a level of obsession to it. Whether it be about school or university grades, or about exercise or weight, it is never going to help us, because no one can be 100% perfect all the time, in every single aspect of their lives. You will fall short sometimes, and that is ok. What would you say to a friend in the same position? If they get a 90% mark, are you going to tell them they're not good enough? That they are simply, not OK, because they fell a bit short of 100%. Even if they got 30%, does that affect their worth? Of course it doesn't. Therefore, a perfectionistic streak, and an eating disorder run on the same tracks. I see them both as entities that are cruel and mean to us. Would we ever subject our loved ones to that kind of thing? The answer would be no, I'm sure. So, why do we subject ourselves to this? Because we have lost the control. We need to get the control back. And we do this, dear readers, by separating this entity from our unique, beautiful, deserving souls, and putting up a fight. And how do we do this? By building up the worth of our unique, deserving souls. By listening to what it has to say, what it wants, what it needs, what is important, and what it truly deserves in this one precious life.

## Functions of an eating disorder... what is its purpose?

When I was a little girl, I wanted to be happy when I grew up. What happened though (and it happened fast), was that, even at the age of 11, I learnt that appearances mattered, and that being thin was good, and overweight, bad. At the age of 11, I went on my first diet, and I somewhat enjoyed this obsession with fat grams and calories. And I did get positive feedback about my small amount of weight loss. My (eventual) eating disorder, was not yet fully activated though, I continued to live my life at the age of 11 or 12, in the best way I knew how. This didn't last though unfortunately, as when I entered high school and ran into some growing pains... teasing and rejection... I turned to the one thing I knew would assist. I went back on a diet, and relatively quickly, this dieting behaviour took over, and then by the time I was 14, it took over completely.

What I am getting at here, and trying to illustrate, is that I was sinking, drowning... I was alone, scared and everything seemed out of my control. I was powerless to stop all the hurt and drama, and I felt worthless. So, my eating disorder, in a manner of sorts, provided some safety, and some distraction from the pain.

When we start to reflect on the purpose of an eating disorder, I feel like it's very important to look at it with a slightly different lens. I feel that it is important not just to look at it entirely as the feared enemy, but in fact, almost an ally, a way of existing that made sense at the time. It came to save us. It gave us a life raft. Seeing the eating disorder as something that initially served us, is helpful. Because then we realise, it is not something to be feared, we must instead try to reassure it, that we no longer need its protection and safeguarding. The reasons it came into existence in the beginning was to protect us, when we were sinking and felt completely worthless. It gave us a focus, something we could control, a way to feel better and a distraction from the woes of life (and in my case, from the woes of growing up). Its purpose was to make us feel worthy, the desire to be thin gave us a way to exist, successfully. We could at the very least, feel good about that. It wasn't until a bit later we started to realise that we essentially lost that sense of control, as the ED took over. Still just trying to make us whole and just OK. To simply survive.

As I said above, I think it is helpful to see your ED essentially as an ally (at least partially). That way we hold less fear towards it. It came to save us when we were scared, alone and vulnerable, but what has happened is that we have grown and learnt and realised that our future self does not need this controlling entity to keep us safe. It has actually turned out to be the opposite, as the ED has grown into something bigger and louder, and now, it is something we have to let go of, so *we* can get the power back. So, we must reassure this part of us (separate but a part of), that we have grown up, and we have started to remember who we are, and our innate worth and value. The ED still hijacks our unique spirit and insists on taking us in a direction that we don't wish to go. If we want to follow our own goals and values… if we want to follow what we know is important to us, then the grip, and the direction our ED wants to take us, must be completely loosened and let go of. The obsession with weight has to stop. But let's reassure this part of us, that we aren't 11 years old anymore, and that we are strong enough to navigate life without its assistance, obsessiveness and control.

See this part of us (the ED) as what it is. It is scared, vulnerable, highly strung and anxious, because it thinks we need it to survive and to just be ok. So, tell it, thank you for being an ally of sorts, but reassure it that you've grown and learnt enough to now navigate this thing called life, on your own. You are no longer that scared, vulnerable 11-year-old, that feels completely alone and worthless. You are starting to reclaim your power by doing this internal work, and your actual survival (the real, unique you) depends on this part of you, finally loosening its grip.

# Utilising eating disorder traits in a positive way

This morning, I realised that whilst the ED part of myself came to help me survive when I was a young girl, and it served its purpose for quite some time (up until... well, recently...), I do not need it anymore. I have found my inner strength over the years, I have found myself, found Kate, and I have solidified myself as a strong, resilient and courageous 41-year-old woman. She is just battling with different parts of self, right now, and she temporarily forgot that she does, indeed, hold the power and reigns to her own life. There is another part of Kate to acknowledge here. The part of me that is wounded, that little girl who was lost and had no sense of self-esteem or self-worth when she was a mere 11 years old, was the part that needed the ED part to survive. She needed it as a life raft when she was sinking in life and in her world. This vulnerable part is still inside Kate, and she is still afraid. And this ED part of Kate is doing her utmost to protect this little girl... by exerting its controlling and obsessive ways onto her. The ED part wants to help this little girl by making damn sure that she stays thin, and therefore protected and immune to life's pain, hurt and unpredictability. If the ED part controls the little girl, it believes it has done its job as protector. At the end of the day, what this little girl actually needs is Kate, the 41-year-old woman who can handle anything that life throws at her and knows who she is and what's important in life. She needs Kate to take her hand and lead her to a happier place, a happier existence, where the little girl can experience joy and freedom. She needs Kate to comfort her and help her relinquish all the fear and pain that has built up over the years, inside of her. I visualise this small little girl, almost in foetal position, swimming into the ocean, with Kate, holding her hand the entire time... I visualise her swimming freely and letting the fear and pain wash gently out of her soul, her entire being. And I see the ED part of Kate appearing relieved, knowing that the little girl is going to be kept safe and protected, without its involvement and its controlling, obsessive ways. At the end of the day, whilst the ED part is terrified of losing its control, it can embrace a new perspective. Whilst it is not needed anymore in the way it has been presenting, when Kate was a little girl, an adolescent, and recently as a grown woman, it is still needed. It has traits and qualities that make this part of self productive and effective in an adult world. Kate doesn't have to banish it completely. All three parts (along with others) can live in peace and harmony. With the little girl being nourished and nurtured and no longer afraid, with Kate living her best life as the strong, together and self-loving woman she has blossomed into and with the ED part of self, putting its determination, grit and persistence into action in healthier ways, there is inner alignment and a sense of harmony and peace within. No longer a very potent, sense of inner conflict.

So, when we look at the ways in which the ED can use its inherent positive traits or qualities in Kate's life to actually better her life and her situation, it is important to firstly identify what some of these positive traits are. And we must firstly explore how they currently present in Kate's life and world. I feel though that obsession needs to go. It is too extreme, and I don't feel that it would do anyone any good if it was to keep presenting in anyone's life. It is an unhealthy trait as such.

However, when we look at the other side of the coin, we can see some traits that may, in fact, be helpful to Kate (and yourself, dear reader), moving forward.

The ones that immediately come to mind are:

**DETERMINATION**
*the quality of being determined, firmness of purpose.*

How does determination currently present in Kate's life, or in your life, dear reader? It presents itself as a kind of firmness in regard to managing weight, with restrictive patterns or excessive exercise. The ED is determined to make us thinner, and we find a sense of resolve to find solutions for weight loss or weight maintenance. Once we find ourselves and remember what is actually important to us (not just being thin, but things that are in line with our personal values and goals), we need to flip this sense of determination on its head. No longer will we strive for thinness, but only for health and happiness. And we can be determined about this.

Our purpose from here on in has now changed, when we start to navigate the journey of recovery. Our purpose now is to keep trying to find who we truly are, and what truly matters, and then go after our hopes and dreams with courage and a sense of passion. We must allow ourselves to embrace a sense of determination moving forward, and our ED can help us with this. The ED has probably continued to be extremely determined in its approach to managing weight over many years, and now, as I said, you must flip it on its head, for the sake of your recovery. I, myself, have known determination for many years in regard to managing my weight, and it has been difficult and very trying. Yet, I kept going, always venturing towards further weight loss. When I was 16 at Hollywood clinic, when I was first recovering from anorexia, it took me some time to process this positive transition, from unhealthy determination to healthy determination. But as I started to get a small taste of freedom, my direction started to change, and my determined approach to weight loss, morphed into a determined approach to life and recovery. Once we can flip the coin, we can truly feel empowered and grateful that we indeed have access to this determination inside ourselves, to use in healthier and more positive ways.

### PERSEVERANCE
*persistence in doing something despite difficulty or delay in achieving success.*

Perseverance is another trait that comes to mind. Which, when utilised in a healthy way, can be very beneficial. Perseverance keeps us going when we run into issues. In the case of eating disorders, perseverance keeps us focused on becoming thin, even when we run into issues with that happening. As I said, though, when utilised properly, in different aspects of your life other than weight loss... this absolutely can set you up for success in many different contexts. There is an element of perseverance that is basically about not giving up. So, when you are out there, living your life, navigating life with all its challenges, perseverance is vital. This could be in relation to a career path, or physical health in general (not weight loss) or trying to find your perfect partner. It is inevitable we will run into roadblocks and diversions in life, so again, flip perseverance on its head and use it for your actual benefit, rather than just weight loss.

With perseverance under your belt, you will be unstoppable.

**PERFECTIONISM**
*refusal to accept any standard short of perfection*

The last ED trait that we need to delve into, is perfectionism.

Perfectionism keeps us driven to achieve a high standard. We won't settle for anything less. When it comes to how this trait presents itself within the realm of your ED, it really isn't a positive thing. It makes us incredibly unhappy if we don't achieve perfection in a weight loss sense. And, as we all know, this perfectionistic trait keeps building our desire to be thin, to the point where this desire will never stop presenting itself. Continued weight loss is of course going to lead to major health issues, even fatality, and it will also lead to your ED taking and maintaining its control over you. Like I have mentioned already, when you feed your ED with negative thoughts and negative behaviours (which is what perfectionism drives us to do), it simply gets bigger and *louder*, and the *control* it has over us gets amplified.

Now, when I first thought this perfectionism thing through, I struggled to see any kind of positive, even in other contexts. But the more I thought about it, when utilised in a certain way, I began to see that yes, there are ways that perfectionism can be of benefit to us. I still think that in many ways it is unhealthy to aim for perfection, because essentially it may make us unhappy if and when we don't achieve 'perfection'. But here is the thing, it doesn't have to make us unhappy if and when we don't achieve 'perfection'. It can be a good thing to aim for – particularly when you look at the context of employment and doing a job that emphasises success – but we can, at the same time as aiming for perfection, be kind to ourselves if we don't get there. You can strive for success, but it doesn't have to affect you in a negative way if you don't get to a standard that you're happy with. It will mean you keep striving, and achieving higher standards as time goes on, which is a fantastic thing, but not getting there doesn't have to affect your self-worth or general happiness on any given day. Let yourself off the hook, and reiterate to yourself that your best is *enough*. But keep striving for success – that is still a positive and healthy approach to life in general. So, again, flip perfectionism on its head, and use it in different ways that are actually of great benefit.

Even I, now (still navigating this ED journey), have a much healthier relationship to perfectionism than I used to. I am kind to myself, and I emphasise that my best is absolutely enough in any context, but I am still using this perfectionistic streak to my benefit. In my work, and in my relationships, particularly. I didn't settle for anything less than perfect in my career and also my romantic relationship with my partner. And I am very happy I set such high standards for myself in these areas. The only thing I still am working on is perfectionism in relation to my appearance and weight. But I am getting there. And you will too, dear reader. And once you flip perfectionistic tendencies on its head, you will be able to navigate life in a much healthier way.

## • What message is your eating disorder sending?

Today I had a thought. We have explored a little bit about the characteristics of an eating disorder, and we have looked at whether our eating disorder should be considered as an enemy or ally (which I am still exploring within myself to be honest); but at the very core of everything, have we considered what message our eating disorder sends us on a daily basis? When you really reflect on this, it is mind-blowing. This is where I come back to the understanding that it is something to be hated. When you think about what it says to us, we realise how cruel the messages are. Today, I had a bad day in relation to my ED. Again, after stepping on the scales and seeing a number I was unhappy with, I freaked out, and this essentially ruined my whole day, as the ED was saying such nasty things. At its very essence it tells me how disgusting I am, which translates to feeling fat and ugly. Straight away, I am no longer the strong, together 41-year-old woman that I am at my core. I am back to feeling like I did when I was 11 years old, when I highly doubted my worth and essentially, my innate value. I know that rationally, what the ED is saying is not true, but rational thought does not even come into it. When the loud ED takes over, rational thought gets completely drowned out. What other messages is it sending us? That we are not ok if we are not thin enough, we are not enough, if we are not thin enough. And the scary thing about eating disorders, is the fact that we will never be thin enough. There will always be one more kg to lose. How is it possible that someone who has actually found their unique self and has worked on self-love and self-esteem endlessly over recent years, can essentially throw all this growth and learning away on any given day, by simply stepping on the scales. Because ED's drown out everything else; all the good things; the good things just don't matter when the ED begins to yell and scream at us that we are not enough...that we are not ok....

So, when it comes to the question of whether our ED's should be viewed as an enemy or an ally, I think we have to separate the parts of ourselves again, to see things clearly. There is the cruel, mean ED part (the enemy), which is telling us how to feel on any given day, depending on what the number is on the scales. There is another side to this ED part though, it is the part that has taken on responsibility of keeping us thin, the part that is "protecting" the wounded 11-year-old girl (in my case). This side to the ED is simply exhausted. This is the part we can see with some empathy and compassion. It has been our (ally), serving a purpose, keeping the wounded 11-year-old safe and protected from the pain and unpredictability of life. Of course, the wounded little girl is the part of us that truly needs nurturing and nourishment, and the only one that can give her that love and nurturing is the unique self, who we are at our core. In my case, it is Kate, the strong, resilient and wise self, that must help this 11-year-old vulnerable part. We...Kate and the little girl, need to stand up to the enemy; and reassure the ally, that they are no longer needed – they don't need to protect the wounded part anymore. Kate essentially has found wholeness; she has grown up and can handle life now. I will say to you, dear reader, that if this is not yet your experience, if you still haven't entirely familiarized yourself with who *you* actually are *without* your ED, this book will give you the outlook, mindset and tools to do so. This part of the journey (finding your unique self) is where the fun begins. Oh, you have so much to look forward to, dear reader.

## • Let's talk about body image – distorted body image and its impacts

One thing that sometimes doesn't occur to me, because I am still somewhat in the grips of an ED, is how very often it seems that not only are we intensely critical of our appearance when affected by an ED, but we just aren't seeing what other people see. We, see ourselves through, shall I say, a very blurry lens. Our vision is somewhat distorted, and we judge ourselves way too harshly. This is not just vision though; in my experience it is also a *feeling*. This indeed, gets amplified if our body weight reduces to an extreme level; I do believe it has been noted that when someone is very underweight, it somehow affects our ability to see things properly. Which, to be honest, still baffles me. But that doesn't mean this isn't 100% true. Eating disorders are, let's remember, a mental illness. I can say with absolute certainty that this was the case for me when I was severely underweight. I, without a shadow of a doubt, felt like I was obese, and when I was forced to gain weight in hospital, it was at the point of being traumatic, because of those "fat", "disgusting" feelings.

This phenomenon is very hard to navigate; and it is *extremely* difficult for others to understand what we are going through, because their lens isn't blurry, like ours is. I think, regardless of your weight (which doesn't matter, remember?) it is important to remind ourselves that we are literally seeing things incorrectly. It is almost as if we need to jolt ourselves back to a sense of reality. I think that this is all that we can do, initially anyway. Once you are on the road to taking back the reins of your life (after reading this book hopefully), and once you start getting to a healthier weight (which is what we need to do to completely recover – which may take some time), it is exceedingly important to continue to check in with your *'why'* of recovery. Why am I wanting to recover? Why am I taking back the controls to my life? *What is important and what isn't*, moving forward? Every time the ED part of you, judges and criticizes your appearance, what must enter, then is your rational self, the *healthy* part, the *whole* part. In my case, the true, unique Kate. The 41-year-old woman who is wise, courageous and resilient beyond measure.

Only Kate can help me to navigate this. The ED part of us is trying to control and obsess – even if its intentions are good (or at least, used to be good), the ED cannot find rational thought, so Kate must do this. The ED part wants to protect us by criticizing us and keeping us motivated to lose weight and control everything. We desperately need to stop buying into this process. What we need to invest in is our *whole* selves, the *real you. The healthy you.* Because this whole part can tell us the truth. We are not fat or disgusting... we are healthy and happy. Well, we will be moving forward, once the ED has loosened its grip. You may need constant 'truth reminders' initially, though.

So, aside from a reminder of the truth, to jolt us back to reality... what else do we need to navigate this issue to a point where it is not an issue anymore?

Unfortunately, I do not have the best news here. I have resigned myself to the fact that there *may* always be a very small part of me that is critical of my appearance, so what must be done is an absolute 360-degree turn around. You need to invest time and energy into *yourself*.... Showing self-love, self-compassion and self-acceptance. It can be done. I have done a lot of work in this area myself over the years, but I am at the point now where I am needing to undertake a lot more of this kind of work, within myself, to find peace again. You will find peace, dear reader, and every time that ED part of you arks up, you can quickly and decisively put it back in its place. You can mute it. You may have to do this for some time before it becomes more natural. And I am still working on this.

It's that *feeling* that is the toughest thing to kick. And I am still navigating that. I will keep you posted on my progress in this area, because I know one thing… We don't deserve to feel fat, disgusting or ugly. And we ARE NOT. Remember, this is how cruel our ED can get, in an effort to remain in control. So, please, you must keep standing up to your ED part, and stay rational and very, very kind to yourself. The vulnerable little girl inside of us needs that love, care and kindness. She does not deserve any less than that.

I am just going to say one more thing in relation to the impacts of this distorted body image. It will keep us stuck, because that is what the ED wants. It wants control and obsession. This is probably the biggest battle we will face with an ED…. It's one thing to find yourself and know who you are and what you want for your future, but the decision to get back into the driver's seat, isn't complete, without addressing the issues with body image. If anyone can tell you it is possible to overcome this, it is me. Whilst I am still fighting a bit of a battle, I have gotten to a point in my life where the ED was conquered, some years ago now. I just need to get back there… and honestly, it's the body image stuff that still manages to keep me stuck in control and obsession, but I will get there, mark my words. You have to be strong enough to fight this battle, and it will take courage and resilience… and some inner work – which you have already begun. I will be exploring how to find that courage and resilience in a later chapter. Hang tight, it's almost time.

# CHAPTER 3
## MOVING FORWARD

### • The Christmas Experiment

I thought I would do the right thing this Christmas and work on not being obsessed with my weight on a daily basis. I would normally weigh myself daily (something I am still working on) and I know from past experience I put on a little bit of weight during Christmas/new year holidays, because the healthy part of Kate realises that everybody indulges a bit at this time of year, and that she too, deserves to relish in the joy of Christmas food and drinks. This Christmas I made the decision to not weigh myself daily. I went for 8 days with no weighing, Christmas Eve to New year's Day. But what happened really took me aback and made me realise how much this thing still has a hold over me. I look at it as great insight and learning, even though it was painful. Oh, so painful. I was ok for about 3 days, and then I could literally feel the weight gain. I could *feel* every ounce of it, just like I could back in my severe anorexic days. I felt so uncomfortable, and I was convinced I had gained at least 5 kgs. It isn't rational, and I am aware of this, but rational thought did not help. I was *convinced*. To the point where it was ruining my holiday. The only thing that kept me somewhat sane is that I absolutely went crazy at the gym; in fact, there were only 3 days out of about 2 weeks that I missed the gym. This made me feel a little bit more 'in control', but I was out of control. My eating disorder swallowed me whole for about 5 days in succession. It took the reins, and I seemed to be powerless to stop it. On the 8th day, I stepped on the scales only to realise that I had gained not even a kg and a half. The relief was huge, but again, I was to realise how there was a little bit of 'anorexia' inside me, still playing its game. Even though I am not really underweight, I kept getting comments from people about how slim/thin I looked, but I can tell you, just like when I was severely anorexic, I didn't believe what they were saying for a nano-second. I saw fat, and I felt fat.

Yes, I have a long way to go. So, lets reflect for a second. I have done a lot of work around knowing who Kate (healthy Kate) really is, what is actually important to her and what goals she wants to achieve etc. And let me tell you, this definitely helps. I can separate the eating disorder from Kate and I can recognise when the ED is taking the reins. But it still has a hold over me. The only thing that quietens it down, is weighing myself daily, because I can see rationally where I am at. I know that I am at a slim, healthy weight, but take the scales away, my head goes rampant. I don't see things clearly, I 100% catastrophise. It is almost as if getting on the scales tells me how to feel on any given day, and what to work towards for that day etc. When I don't weigh myself, I simply don't know how to feel. This is extremely problematic.

So how, dear reader, can we navigate this. I get taken back to when I was at Hollywood Clinic, where they weighed us all twice a week, to make sure our weight was increasing to a point that was more healthy. This was just as hard back then. So how did I get through this? And how can I replicate that experience now? The thing that I keep coming back to, is that you need people you can trust, to be that rational voice, to tell you that you are beautiful, to tell you that your weight doesn't actually matter in the scheme of things. I feel as if it is extremely important to lean on others at this time. So, for me, now, I talk to my partner, talk to my trusted friends, and I know that there will be a stage that is very uncomfortable, as we navigate through the issue with weighing/not weighing. I have landed back in a similar position to where I was at 25 years ago. And really, I am actually in a much better position than I was back then. I don't have to completely rebuild myself and my whole life, as I already know who Kate is, what Kate wants and needs, and Kate has an abundance of wonderful relationships and friendships to support her through this journey. Back then, everything was a clean slate completely, which is an amazing thing, but also very daunting. As I was walking ahead on faith alone, that everything would turn out ok, or better than ok even. I have done so much of the work that needs to be done, already. It simply (or not quite so simply in fact) comes back down to the weight obsession, and the habit of weighing myself on a daily basis. Why am I finding this so damn difficult?

At the end of the day, right now, I don't have a doctor and a treating team calling the shots, I am only accountable to myself, the decision to weigh myself daily, is a habitual, obsessive thing, and as someone who years ago, experienced extreme OCD, I truly understand how unhelpful and downright awful, obsessiveness can become, when you let it rule your life.

So, dear reader, if you are in a similar boat, let's do this together. I will make a pact to work on this inherent obsessiveness and look at cutting down the act of jumping on the scales every morning. I think we need to remember, that like with any addiction, it is going to be a battle, at least in the very beginning. It is going to feel uncomfortable, to say the least, but we must remember this won't last forever, so we must simply ride that wave of uncomfortableness. As someone who has worked with clients as an alcohol and drug counsellor, and I think it might be helpful to view eating disorders as an addiction of sorts. Like I said earlier in the book, this addiction can get in the way of our goals and in the way of being the sort of person we wish to be. Realising this is huge. But actually, ceasing the addictive behaviour, is the absolute hardest part. The theory behind it all, can absolutely make sense, but it doesn't just take away all the hard work you must take part in to completely conquer your addiction for good. There will be a lot of discomfort, as we slowly but surely give up our addiction. And in my case, and perhaps yours too, dear reader, it is about giving up that action of jumping on the scales every day. I did this for 8 days over Christmas and new year, and as I said, it was painful; but it was also a valuable learning experience. I know that I can do it, because I did it, I just need to remember that the discomfort will eventually dissipate. It won't last forever. With my clients, I used to talk about the concept of urge surfing. This simply means riding that uncomfortable wave of having an urge or a craving and knowing that it will pass. I think this concept can be used here in a sense. What makes our situation more difficult however is if weighing ourselves is the addiction, our urge to weigh probably won't last 2-3 hours, it starts off by literally affecting your whole day. Over this 8-day period, the feels were there consistently.

This just means, we have to be as solid as a rock in terms of our desire to change. Remember what is important; remember what you're aiming for; and remember your 'why'... as in 'why am I wanting to change'.

This book hopefully will motivate you to really articulate what your 'why' is.... And hopefully it will motivate you to want to change for the better; and become a healthier, happier version of yourself, where your ED isn't calling the shots. If you get up tomorrow and simply skip jumping on the scales, you must be ready for battle. It will be a battle. But I've got this. You've got this. We have got this.

This Christmas and new year period could be looked upon with great disappointment and upset. But I am trying to turn it around. It has motivated me, intrinsically, to change my life. I don't want next Christmas to be a repeat of this one. I am going to beat this obsession with weight, and I am going to win this battle before me.

> "Ruin is a gift. Ruin is the road to transformation"
> Elizabeth Gilbert

Watch this space.

## • When stepping on the scales... take a reality check

Whenever you step on the scales, your ED gets given the opportunity to run riot. When this happens, the number on the scales literally gives your ED the power to dictate your levels of peace, happiness and self-worth on any given day. When you think about it, this is ludicrous. We must stop giving our ED the power. How do we do this? Bluntly remind ourselves of who we are, and what is truly important to us. What we value and treasure in our lives has nothing to do with a number on the scales. We need a reality check... pronto. I would of course encourage you to not step on the scales, however I know this can be very difficult, particularly in the beginning stages of recovery. If you must continue to weigh yourself, I would keep it to a minimum, perhaps weekly. And when you see those numbers flash before you, see them with the eyes of your rational, healthy self. Not through the eyes of your ED. Do not give it the power in this situation, it is vital. Do not listen to its harsh words of obsession, criticism and judgment. You do not deserve that. Noone does.

## • What matters, what doesn't.

I think we can safely say now what matters and what doesn't in our one precious life. When we look at those simple words, One. Precious. Life. This pretty much sums it up. It points towards the fact that you only have *one* life in your unique soul, your body and your presence. There is only one *you*. And there is only one life – as *you*. What is going to matter at the end of your one precious life? What will you remember? What will you be grateful for? For me, I can say with 100% certainty, that I will be grateful for the wonderful memories, the laughs that I have shared with those I love, the fun we've had, the adventures we've had and the love that was shared. I don't want to get to the end of my one precious life and realise I spend way too much time worried about my appearance or weight. Because, at the end of the day, these things don't matter one bit. We need to be grateful for our body and our health, rather than punishing it or constantly criticizing it. This is because our bodies are the vehicle that takes us through this ride called life, and not everyone is so lucky to have a functioning vehicle. When you are battling with your ED, it's ok to fight back with the argument that ED's (whilst they came to us initially to help us) are pointless. We are just wasting our precious time and energy, by focusing incessantly on weight and appearance. You can thank your ED for its initial assistance, but again, then let it know that you have bigger fish to fry. You have so much inner potential (you may be yet to realise this entirely), to reach for the stars and achieve your hopes and dreams, but this is not how things will play out if we keep the ED in the driver's seat.

I am going to mention food here as well. A quote that I love:

> "One of the very nicest things about life, is the way we must regularly stop whatever it is that we are doing, and devote our attention to eating"
> Anon

Ask anyone who doesn't have an ED, whether this is true for them, I guarantee a large portion of them would agree that this is true. Food is meant to be enjoyed and relished. And usually, we enjoy food with other people, and it should be a joyous experience. I can relate to this; I still enjoy going out with my partner and relishing a delicious meal. This is when Kate is in the drivers' seat, and I never regret it. One of the other beautiful things in life, that I will look back on at the end of my life, is the meals I have enjoyed and more than anything else, the meals I have enjoyed with the people I love and care about. ED's can take this joy from us entirely. We deserve to enjoy food as much as the next person, so if you are at a point where food scares you, I am assuming the ED is very much still in the driver's seat, and you have some work to do, which I believe, dear reader, can be started as you read this book and start reflecting on what is actually important.

## • Finding Courage, Hope & Resilience Within

If we are going to beat this thing (which we absolutely are), I can say from my own experience of beating it before, that it is imperative to find within yourself, three things. A good dose of Courage, Hope and Resilience. These three qualities are so incredibly important moving forward, and the good news is this: These are not things that we either have or don't have, these are qualities that can indeed be nurtured within. So that they can be used in a way that is meaningful and powerful for us. Think of it like this... they are untapped resources...there is an endless supply within... we just need to wake up to this truth and access them the best we can, and it does get easier. As the quote at the beginning of the book says – "Struggle is nature's way of strengthening it". In terms of resilience, the great news is that because we go through all these struggles with control, obsession, body image, food and the like; simply getting through the day sometimes is *very* difficult and challenging. But by simply navigating this the best we can, this already builds a certain amount of inner strength or resilience. Once we start getting into the journey of recovery; as hard as it is, we must recognize that this battle is going to make us strong in the end, and we will realise that we will become much more resilient than the 'average' person.

Navigating life can be hard, we all know this. So, the fact that we are going through the throes of a mental illness right now, should (dare I say it) be considered a good thing (in a strange way). Because what we are experiencing will, once we achieve recovery from our ED, make the rest of our lives somewhat richer, more meaningful and it will make the rest of our lives more manageable. As someone who has lived not only through an eating disorder, but also other equally distressing and challenging mental health issues, I can honestly say that my levels of resilience are now sky high. I can bounce back from anything (separate from the ED issues I am still experiencing). In life, simply navigating day to day issues is so much easier for me than some of the other people in my life. I have friends (and family) that simply crumble when something challenging comes their way. For me, challenge is like water off a duck's back (as the saying goes). Sure, resilience doesn't take the challenges away, but it makes them sting a whole lot less, and I can just carry on with my day, relatively unaffected. This can and will be you, dear reader, when you start fighting this battle with your ED, and stand up to it - your strength through struggle, will come. Hang tight. You will experience what I am talking about here, as you take back the reigns and control of your one precious life.

So, know that resilience will come, dear reader, as long as you don't give up. Which we know we won't. Because persistence and perseverance are innate qualities that we already possess, as already discussed. There are two more pieces to the puzzle however, and one of these is hope. Without hope, navigating life literally feels hopeless, and truly giving up, sadly becomes an option.

We need to do our best to always be hopeful, however I know from experience that an ED does its best to take this away from us. So, how do we find hope when we are hopeless? My answer to this should be helpful to you. If we can't manage to find hope (which was the case for me initially when I was going through the throes of anorexia), all that got me through at the time was allowing others to hold the hope for me. How does this work exactly? When other people (friends, family, or even our clinicians) believe in us and our recovery, it can assist us. The more we allow ourselves to listen to their messages of hope and inspiration, things will improve eventually, until you learn to muster that sense of hope for yourself. It took me a long time to see the possibility for change, and when other people would tell me that I was strong enough to beat the ED and move forward towards health and happiness, I resisted this initially.

However, the simple act of reading this book, dear reader, tells me that there is already, a glimmer of hope inside. You are at the very least, entertaining the thought that maybe...just maybe... there is a way out of the pain, and that this is what you really want. Take that small glimmer and continue to do some self-exploration around what you want for your future; separate the ED from who you truly are, and keep daydreaming about things being better, and different. This glimmer of hope that is there, will grow, and the more you take back the reigns and the more you allow yourself to sit yourself in the driver's seat of your life, the easier it will be to access a good dose of hope for yourself. When you have setbacks, or when you're really battling with your ED, this glimmer of hope will keep you strong, and yes... stronger than your ED. Like I said though, if you are still in a hopeless place, dear reader, allow yourself to listen to others' hopeful words, until they start to seep in a bit. What you need is to get to a point where you are truly motivated for change. Once you get to this point, like now with reading this book, things will get much easier. It will be tough, but you are tough enough, dear reader, to get to where you want to be.

> "If you have the courage to begin,
> you have the courage to succeed"
> Anon

When it comes to courage, the last piece of the 3-part puzzle, it is important to recognize that whilst we may not see ourselves as particularly courageous, this is just because we haven't seen it manifest within us yet; it doesn't mean that it is not there, under the surface. We do not necessarily recognise courage until after the fact - we don't know it's there until we have started facing our fears. Once we start engaging in even the smallest courageous acts, we will be able to reflect and see it for what it is. And once you start this process, you will be able to start taking even bigger steps forward. Even if all you can muster today, dear reader, is to challenge your ED by taking a tiny bit of positive action (not weighing self for one day or engaging in self-care, etc) - this is a start. Once you continue to take these small steps, you will then be able to make some real power moves in regard to positive change (start setting goals, be more accepting of help). All these things, while they may seem small, are epic stand up power moves against your ED.

Like the quote refers to, once you can simply begin your courage journey, you can, in essence, become unstoppable. Just see your small courageous acts today, as the start of something so much bigger. Courage, in essence, is simply the willingness to be afraid and act anyway. When you think about it like this, courage is simple. *Feel the fear yet do it anyway.* On a small scale, or on a large scale, it is the same muscles that you are flexing each time. However, the more you flex those muscles (your 'courage muscles') the stronger the muscles will become and the easier it will become to enact change. When it came to my recovery from anorexia, I didn't have any choice but to go to the psychiatric clinic, and like I have said, I completely resisted the process of recovery in the beginning stages. But eventually, through gaining a little bit of hope (that others held for me), I became ready to start challenging my ED. Just a little bit at first, but yes, I did start flexing my courage muscles by starting to eat normal foods at normal times, by eventually letting myself be seen, even when I was at my most vulnerable.

> "Courage starts with showing up and letting ourselves be seen."
> Brene Brown

When you think about it, even imagining your life being different, or daydreaming about a happy life, is in itself a courageous act, because your ED doesn't want you to have this sense of freedom. It wants you to stay 'safely' in its shackles. So, any small – even minute – act that moves you towards recovery is huge, like reading this book, dear reader. Be proud of yourself for even the most minute movements forward. This acknowledgement will make *you stronger* and your *ED weaker*. It will also further strengthen your courage muscles. You can probably begin to see now just how important courage is in our recovery journeys. Because at the end of the day, there is going to have to be *a lot of change*. Don't let this overwhelm you though, because all this change is positive, and the journey itself can be exciting and so rewarding. Yes, change can absolutely be scary, but by flexing your courage muscles, you can move forward exponentially, even if and when fear is present (Remember "feel the fear yet do it anyway).

> **"Change is hard at first, messy in the middle, and gorgeous at the end"**
> Robin Sharma

This positive action to create positive change will also ramp up your levels of strength and resilience, so you truly will be an unstoppable force moving forward.

I talk a lot about courage, hope and resilience in my first book, more in relation to my recovery from my other mental health issues in my late 20s and 30s. I maintain that I would not be where I am in my life, had I not had these 3 ingredients at my core. When anyone is going to be up against challenges and struggles, it is so important to lean on these innate qualities. And when it comes to any journey of mental health recovery (including eating disorders), which generally involves 2 steps forward, 1 step back, and challenges and struggles on a daily basis (in the beginning anyway); it is even more imperative to nurture these life-changing innate qualities. I have had to continuously push myself out of my comfort zone, to rebuild my life (which took huge amounts of courage). I have had to remain hopeful (even when things don't always go to plan) and be my own cheerleader of sorts. I have had to lean on a high level of resilience (which I feel grew strong after my recovery from anorexia).

I truly believe, dear reader, that once you conquer your ED, you will be highly familiarised with these 3 qualities or traits. Because you will need to lean on them and nurture them daily. But the wonderful thing is, you will be well-equipped for the next parts of your journey through life. Successful recovery from an ED comes with huge blessings. And you will get there, dear reader, once you start exploring these key attributes within and utilising them in any way you can.

> "Every experience, no matter how bad it seems, holds within it a blessing of some kind. The goal is to find it"
> Buddha

Build your *resilience*, by standing up against your ED, and taking back your power.

Always hold onto *hope*, even if others need to hold the hope for you in the beginning.

Push your comfort zone consistently, using your *courage* muscles, to rebuild your one precious life, one small step at a time.

## • Building Self-worth & Self-love

I am extremely familiar with the concepts of self-worth and self-love. I have done a lot of work on both over the years. Let's talk about self-worth first. Our ED will tell us that we are not worthy of good things and that we don't deserve a happy, healthy life. We must recognise that this is one of the attributes of an ED, so when it makes you feel this way about yourself, recognise that this is purely false. It is the ED attempting to keep you 'safely' within its shackles. It doesn't want you to get better, it doesn't want you to get healthier, it simply wants you to be thinner. Recognise it for what it is. And separate *yourself* from its harsh feelings and words. Once we can stand separate from it, and once we have realised that we do not need to listen to these cruel, negative words; we can start to look at building up our self-worth. I tend to use inner-child work in relation to this concept. In that, when you think about the young girl you used to be, before an ED came into the picture, you realise how much this little girl deserves. She deserves to be loved, she deserves to be happy, and whole. When you can acknowledge that what you have been doing has not been serving this inner child one iota, we can find some motivation to do things differently. Start seeing yourself as an extension of this pure, loving, kind inner child. Make a pact with yourself that you will start to take more care of this inner child, you will be compassionate, loving and kind towards her, and work towards the happy, healthy life that she so desperately deserves. Once you find that motivation within, there are additional things you can do to ramp up your self-worth. Some of these things might seem simplistic, yet I assure you, they are powerful. 1) Use affirmations to reinforce positive beliefs about yourself. Affirm that you are worthy and deserving. Affirm that you are loveable and kind. Affirm that you are strong, resilient and courageous. 2) Find a sense of purpose by doing what you love. You may well not have any idea about what lights you up in life, as you may not have ever explored it. So, if this is the case, it's time to start exploring this. Really dig deep into your true, authentic self and ask the question, what am I passionate about? For me, it's writing, music and my relationships. This question sets in motion a very positive, exciting and powerful process. Once you know the answer to this, use your courage muscles to build this into your life. You won't regret it. This is literally strengthening *you* and weakening your ED. 3) Learn to accept compliments. One powerful thing you can try to do is accept compliments from others. Our ED automatically resists compliments, because a) if people say you look nice, that just means we're not 'sick' or 'thin' enough. b) our ED automatically filters out any positive from others, because according to our ED, we have no innate positive's. Once you start saying "thankyou" to other people's compliments, this allows self-worth to start creeping in and creeping up. Stand up to your ED and remember, it's ok to say, "thank you". 4) Recognise your accomplishments. What have you done, or achieved in your life that you can be proud of? This feeds and helps build your self-worth. If you can't think of anything, remind yourself that once you conquer your ED, you will be free to accomplish anything you want (and conquering your ED in itself - is a huge accomplishment). Your journey may not have started yet, but remember, all of this self-exploration we are doing, will assist you on your path. 5) Avoid self-criticism. This might seem obvious, but it is imperative to remember this. Because your ED will continue to criticise, and it may try to get stronger and louder whilst you're living your journey of recovery. Powerfully recognise when this is happening and sit yourself back in the drivers' seat. Tell your ED you aren't going to listen to its criticism anymore, because you are indeed, getting stronger and louder yourself. 6) Focus on the good in yourself. Remind yourself constantly that you possess innate positive qualities. When your ED eventually lessens in power, it is important to acknowledge these positives. Nurture them and focus on them, moving forward; and your self-worth will grow.

 Now let's talk about self-love. Some people may have led you to believe that self-love is too fluffy a concept. But in my opinion, it is incredibly relevant. Self-love is basically an attempt at being caring and compassionate towards the self. Just like you would do with someone *you* love, a friend, family member or partner. If someone you love was struggling, you would shower them with kindness, compassion and empathy. The fact that we do the opposite for ourselves does not make sense then. In actual fact, if we are completely loving and compassionate with ourselves, we are much better equipped to look after the ones we love. Think of the analogy "I must first *fill my cup* before I go to help others". This is 100% true and relevant. In fact, the most important relationship we have in this life is the one we have with ourselves. Which is why it's so incredibly pivotal to be our own best friend. If you only help others, but not yourself, you will burn out. Especially if you're struggling yourself with an ED. Your ED drains you of self-love, self-compassion and self-worth. So, in an effort to rid ourselves of our ED and its soul-destroying ways, we must learn to fill our cups, on a daily basis in fact. So, dear reader, how do we fill our cups? This part is crucial. We must engage in self-care. Self-care nurtures and nourishes our very soul, and it is the way to become empowered, and get *your power back*.

> ### "Self-care is how you get your power back"
> #### Lalah Delia

It is also incredibly important to take stock of your levels of self-care moving forward, because here is the thing. With every act of self-care, our authentic self (essentially, *you*), gets stronger, and the critical, obsessive, fearful part of us (essentially our ED) gets weaker. So, what does self-care involve, or look like? It is much more than giving yourself a pedicure or a bubble bath (not that these aren't nurturing activities!) Like I said, it is about engaging in activities that feed our unique soul, and this can look different for each of us. My self-care usually involves having fun with friends, watching *'Friends'* on Netflix, cranking my favourite music, reflective writing, or enjoying a nice, warm latte at a café. There are less obvious self-care strategies, though, which are also extremely important.

This includes setting personal boundaries and being able to say the word 'no' when you don't want or have the energy for something that someone wants you to do. It is anything that meets the requirement of "looking after the self". Listening to your body and taking ownership of your unique sense of wellbeing. Practicing gratitude comes under this umbrella also, because writing or saying things that we are grateful for makes us *feel good*, and appreciative, and feeling like this will also in fact help you attract more good things that you want and/or need (but that in itself is a whole other book that needs writing!) Changing your perspective is another way of taking good care of yourself. So, instead of seeing the glass half empty, try to practice seeing it half full. See your situation from a "growth mindset", instead of a "fixed mindset", where you appreciate your challenges and see them as opportunities to grow, learn and become stronger. This all falls under self-care and taking good care of your wellbeing, moving forward. So, dear reader, what does self-care look and feel like to you? Take your ED out of the equation, because your ED will simply tell you that you don't deserve anything good. Remember that inner child and know that your inner child needs to be nourished and nurtured from this day forward.

One other factor worth noting, is that the way others treat you, also starts with you. If you love and show respect to yourself, others will surely admire this in you. So, if you want *healthy, happy* and *functional* relationships in your life (which is exactly what you deserve), it is imperative that your relationship to self is also *healthy, happy* and *functional*. Self-compassion, self-care and self-love are the answers here.

I have come a long way on my self-love journey, and although I am still somewhat battling a part of my ED, and it is challenging, I also, in general, show myself a fair amount of love and kindness. I look after myself #1. I fill my cup consistently. Because in that way, I can also be a much better friend, daughter, sister and partner.

So, dear reader, to begin with, simply make some small adjustments to fit some nurturing and nourishment into your daily life, as I have already said, these positive activities that help to cultivate self-love and kindness, literally, are like kryptonite to your ED. These things will help empower you and hence disempower (and quieten) your ED.

The fact that you may not have been aware of all of this in the past, and the fact that you may have been falling short of the self-love mark on a consistent basis, is ok. You must forgive yourself and simply vow to change this in the future. You can do it, dear reader; start exploring self-care and being kind to yourself, as you would do to a dear friend. It will change your life in the most incredible way, and it will quieten your ED significantly. Remember to celebrate the small wins along the way, whether this is temporarily quietening down your ED whilst you sing along to your favourite song, or by cooking yourself a nourishing meal, relish in the joy of self-empowerment.

# TELL YOUR EATING DISORDER TO F*** OFF

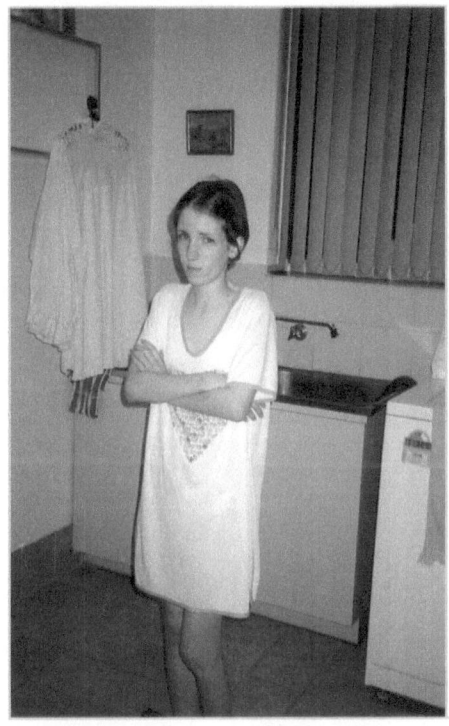

Kate at 14 years old, her parents taking a photo hoping she would see how underweight she was

Kate at 14 years old, Christmas Day with her Mum and sister-in-law. Christmas day was always difficult as it revolves around food and eating

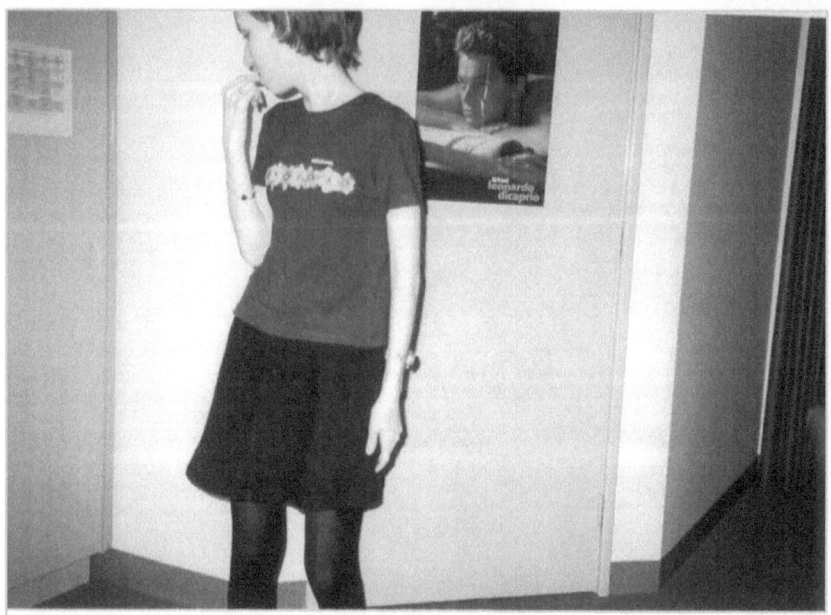

Kate at 15 years old, starting her admission at Hollywood clinic. Kate hated being photographed

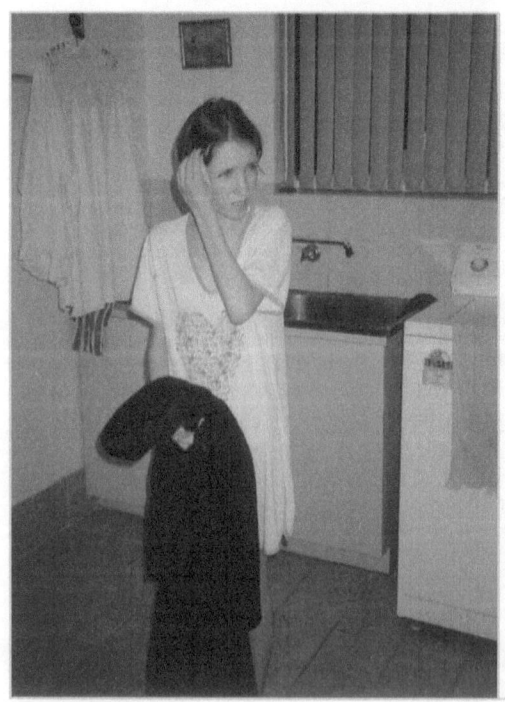

Another photo of Kate at 14 that her parents took

# TELL YOUR EATING DISORDER TO F*** OFF

Kate at 15 years old, before her 9th admission to hospital, weighing only 29kgs

February 2025 – Book Launch for Hope Inc

Fun photoshoot with a friend – August 2024

Leon (the love of my life) and myself at the pub after book launch February 2025

# TELL YOUR EATING DISORDER TO F*** OFF

Leon and I all loved up at our home - February 2025

Leon and I, loved up- photoshoot at Crown for our 6-year anniversary – June 2025

Myself and a good friend, having fun - September 2025

Myself at Crow Books – promoting Hope Inc – Dream come true - February 2025

# TELL YOUR EATING DISORDER TO F*** OFF

Myself all ready and excited
for my 40th birthday party
– November 2024

Myself – having a blast -
best dressed winner for
Melbourne Cup luncheon
– November 2024

# CHAPTER 4
## THE FINAL JOURNEY HOME

### • Back to basics – seeking help to help myself

Throughout the writing of this book (towards the latter end), I must say my ED was winning the battle. I was far too focused on becoming thinner and thinner, and I was not only restricting from Monday-Friday, I was also fasting 2 days a week and going to the gym for intensive workouts (an excessive amount) 4 times per week. My weight was starting to drop, and I was becoming even more obsessed with seeing the numbers go down, and still weighing daily (which is again, obsessive). Until now. Now... I am starting to win. But I will get to that in a bit...

People were starting to comment on my weight loss, and I instinctively knew that I needed, in some way, to fight back. One of my friends gave me the name of a psychologist who specialises in eating disorders, and I felt like this was a good start – I actually came to the realisation that I didn't want to keep going down this path (*step 1*). So, in my first session with the psychologist, I got her up to speed with everything. She asked me to complete an eating disorder questionnaire, which came back indicating that I am indeed experiencing atypical anorexia, with my obsession with weight and restrictive behaviours, which floored me. Never did I think I would get to this place again. What started as a relatively healthy goal, eventually turned into an eating disorder. But that gave me motivation to do something about it. About 3 months ago.

The psychologist swiftly suggested I see a dietician, and that I should probably put on some weight, so one of my close friends gave me the details of a dietician who specialises in eating disorder recovery. I was scared shitless, but I knew that I needed professional help...a nudge in the right direction. The first session with the dietician was interesting, but really just getting her up to speed on my situation – with antipsychotic medication and such. In further sessions, the dietician explained that I was more than likely quite malnourished, and we had to have a close look at my diet. She, too, mentioned that gaining a few kilos would be a good thing, and that I eventually needed to stop the daily weighing. It was after the third session that I started making changes and making headway. Again, I was petrified of gaining weight, but she told me to trust in my body. The moment I started to nourish my body – introducing more food and particularly carbohydrates and grain foods, I started to realise how malnourished I was prior to this. I had more energy, more focus, and I was less exhausted by the end of the day.

Eventually, we made the goal of weighing weekly instead of daily – which was super scary – particularly when I knew I struggled with this last Christmas - but I knew I needed to become much less obsessed with the numbers. And we also made the goal of stopping the fasting, as it was far too restrictive and really fed my eating disorder and its controlling ways. It was time to stand up to the ED and make some very positive changes. I started to feel like I was ready for change. And I literally kept telling myself – change is hard at first, messy in the middle, but beautiful at the end. This became my daily mantra. When I started to weigh weekly instead of daily, something shifted. I was immediately less obsessive – the only thing was though – I noticed I was body checking a lot more – looking in mirrors and reflections, etc. Which is something I will be working on with both the dietician and psychologist, moving forward.

I am not out of the woods yet, but I have definitely turned a corner over the past 3 months. I have put on a little bit of weight – but it has evened out – and I am feeling much better for it. The desire to be thin is waning – it is becoming far less intense – and the new goal is being healthy. I feel like I am eating a lot, but I understand that this is what my body desperately needs. I am literally telling my ED to stick it – every morning when I choose not to weigh myself, and every time I nourish my body with good food and nutrition – I am *choosing wellness (and balance)* instead. Kate is getting back in the driver's seat. I am reaching out more to friends who are keeping me accountable and getting support from my family and my partner. I have also found that all the messages in this book – have been very helpful in my recovery – as I hope is the case for you, dear reader. However, I also encourage you to seek out professional help if and when you need it. I needed a push in the right direction, and I am so happy I sought help before things got any worse.

More than anything else, I now have oodles more hope, that I can kick this thing to the kerb for good. I also have hope for you, dear reader, with the messages and tools that you can find in this book, and maybe with a bit of professional help – particularly around food – I know *you* can do this. We can do this. Remember the first step in your journey is to make that clear-cut decision - to tell your eating disorder to F*** off. This is when the work begins. I indeed made that decision – but it happened gradually – it wasn't an overnight revelation. Let hope seep in. *Choose wellness and balance over obsession and control.* And always remind yourself of *your why.*

> **FOR LOVED ONES:** Do what you can to encourage your loved one to seek professional help – I believe particularly with a dietician who specialises in eating disorders. We must fight the battle, but often we may need assistance with the practicalities involved – what our diet should look like and also the challenge of navigating weight gain and eventually choosing not to step on those scales.

## • Malnourishment Vs Nourishment and Healing

This chapter of the book is not exactly something that I planned on having at the beginning. I honestly had no idea how malnourished I had been over the past couple of years, particularly this last year – until I started seeing the dietician and taking stock of what I eat on a daily basis. Like I said before, the moment I started making positive changes to my diet - and more than anything else, increasing carbohydrates (which I used to dread) and grain foods- was the moment I realised how important re-feeding and nourishment can be in your overall recovery from an eating disorder. There is a nutritional component to restrictive eating disorders. Starving your body starves your brain as well, and this affects your perception and your thinking. You literally become more obsessive and more self-critical – and much more focused on losing weight - I have experienced this recently – I have experienced the dramatic change with the simple (well, maybe not so simple – but every bit worth it) act of nourishing my body with adequate nutrition. So, in your journey back to health, dear reader, try to remember how important it is to feed your body adequately. If this is too difficult to tackle alone, then seek professional help – as I did – to make you accountable and to give you a gentle nudge in the right direction. I am no dietician – but to make a quick note – your diet should have enough of each of the main food groups – including fruit, vegetables, grains, protein and dairy. And hey, you know what? I am trying to enjoy eating all the extra foods – which really does tell my eating disorder to get F***ed!

## • Loosening its grip

I am getting a sense now – and this is very important – that my eating disorder is loosening its grip. I still have a way to go, dear reader, but as I said, I am making incredible headway –

and being thin is slowly becoming much less important. Being happy and well is paramount, though, which therefore means that the eating disorder has to go. With good nutrition and less obsession over the number on the scales – I do really feel like 'Kate' is getting back into the driver's seat. I have noticed that I am actually more patient and kinder to others – and I am able to focus on other goals that are much more aligned with who I want to be as a person. The amount of time I spent every day, obsessing over the number on the scales and obsessing over food, was considerable – and pointless. I have so much more time to do other things now! There are never enough hours in the day, so why on earth would you waste countless minutes and hours thinking about something that actually doesn't matter one iota? Instead… think about your goals and your dreams and start manifesting the life that you desire! That is indeed time well spent – rather than wasting time on a number.

## • Reminders of who I am and what is important to me

One thing that is making this whole recovery process a lot easier is simply reminding myself on a daily (sometimes hourly) basis of what is important to Kate. I need to remind myself that being thin is not actually important – but that being healthy, happy, fulfilled and free are the most important things. Physical health is now something that I will stay on top of. I am still going to the gym for fitness and the endorphins, but I am eating a nourishing diet now and making sure I have good nutrition. Happiness comes from my relationships, friendships, simply moving forward towards my goals and dreams and upping the self-care practices. Fulfilment comes from my work in mental health, as well as writing and speaking. Freedom is what I have been experiencing in relation to my eating disorder – I am breaking free – and this is only going to get better. Reading through this manuscript is very helpful too, particularly when looking at my personal values. Kate values kindness, fun, authenticity and connection. And to be fair, all of these values were falling by the wayside whilst my eating disorder was causing havoc in my life. So again, I encourage you, dear reader, to remind yourself consistently what is important and what is not. Remind yourself of the person you want to be and what you want your life to look like moving forward. You may never have experienced the sense of freedom that you get once you tell your eating disorder to F*** off. But this is something to look forward to! You've got this!

> FOR LOVED ONES: Remind your loved one of their amazing qualities, outside of their eating disorder, remind them of who they are – and who they have always been. Remind them of their inner child and what she/he deserves.

## • Kate is back in the driver's seat

I am in the process of getting Kate back in the driver's seat. I am not 100% there yet, but I have no doubt I will be kicking this thing to the kerb – for good - in the near future. I want to get to the point where I am comfortable just weighing myself monthly and just trust that my body will end up where it is meant to. I have come so far in 3 months already, so I imagine in another few months I will have freedom at last. I don't want an eating disorder to be a part of my life moving forward, and whilst this is going to be challenging, it will be 100% worth it in the end.

I want to focus on my goals in other areas of my life. I want to get engaged to my partner, I want to travel, and I want to pursue more challenging and rewarding work. I also want to publish this book and my next book 'Level Up' and even consider writing a 4th book. I want to do a TEDx talk – I actually got down to the top 20 in 2017 but just missed the cut as they only took 16. I have many messages to get out there in the world. Not only about recovery from eating disorders, but mental health recovery in general, and how people experiencing mental health challenges are immeasurably resilient, which will be of great benefit to them once they recover. I believe that once you have been through a mental health challenge and made it to the other side, you will be more passionate, more gritty and more grateful for the little things and the big things. Remember this, dear reader, you are indeed, immeasurably resilient. Battling with an eating disorder is extremely difficult and will test your strength, but once you've kicked it to the kerb, you will literally be unstoppable.

# CHAPTER 5
## FINAL NOTES

### • Balance, not addiction, or obsession

I have learnt that what we want to aim for is balance in our lives when it comes to food and weight, etc, instead of addiction or obsession. And I am well on the way.

So, what does balance look and feel like, in the grand scheme of things? You have to know what balance feels like, in your body, and compare that to what obsession and addiction feel like, in your body. Obsession is a heavy load to carry around on a daily basis. It's exhausting. Balance feels much lighter and is much more palatable. Every morning when you wake up, prioritise balance in your life. Tell your ED to stick it.

Start your day in that way. You will be able to *feel* it when you start obsessing. And you will *feel* it when you find balance. If you are off kilter, you will notice that, and you can do something about it. If you need to weigh yourself in the morning, do so (preferably not), but write the number down on a piece of paper, and then tear it up. That is the last moment you will allow yourself to think about your weight, all day. If and when you notice the obsessive thoughts coming in, simply remind yourself of *your* priorities. Your priorities are focusing on what is *actually important* in your life (as you have already discovered, earlier in this book), and your priorities moving forward are also seeking *balance, health, happiness* and *harmony*. Remind yourself that you are 100% deserving of a balanced, healthy, happy and harmonious life. Harmonious = forming a pleasing or consistent whole. Remember that is what we are aiming for!! And guess what? It is not too common to completely achieve a sense of harmony in one's life. Therefore, once you have this nailed, you will be ahead of the game, and unstoppable!

I feel like this thing called balance, is definitely on the horizon for me...and the biggest hurdle I had to jump was cutting back the weighing – but I have done that, and I feel amazing *and empowered*. I know you can do this too, dear reader. I refuse to let a number take up way too much space in my mind, body and soul. I don't want to be an obsessive person any more.... It's so incredibly unhealthy, and it was simply making me far more stressed and miserable than I needed to be.

When you stress and obsess about a number, your eating disorder is in the driver's seat and your eating disorder is trying to take control. Simply don't let it, simply remind yourself of who *you* are, and what is *actually important*.

There is nothing healthy about obsession. It is your eating disorder.... 100%. Do not let it win this battle. Stay strong. Literally tell your ED to shove it – and don't step on those scales!

Balance requires taking a step back and viewing the situation with rational thought. Step back, breathe, and then move forward. You will be so proud of yourself for taking a stand against your ED. Every time that you stand up to it, you are grabbing your power back; you are putting up a fight. Be proud and reward yourself- buy yourself some flowers or have a good laugh. *Take back your power and embrace happiness and health. Empower yourself.*

You're not alone, dear reader, I am on this journey with you. We will do this together.

And with the space that is freed up in your mind, body and soul, when you let go of obsessing, you can fill it with positive, healthy and exciting things! Grab your life back by the horns and begin to explore who *you* want to be, moving forward and what *you* want *your* life to look like. This can be an exciting process. Remember, you have a clean slate to start working with. Prioritise balance and I guarantee things will start to shift, even if it is a battle at first, you are more than capable of winning this fight. No one else can do this for you. It is up to *you*. With the tools and concepts explored in this very book, you can start to begin your journey to freedom.

I want you to also do a quick meditation and visualisation – every day:

I want you to simply breathe... and then visualise a life where you are balanced and whole. I want you to feel into what that feels like and see what that looks like.

I want you to affirm to yourself that you are balanced, healthy, happy and whole. I want you to affirm to yourself that you live with a sense of peace and harmony.

Do this for ten minutes, every morning, and add in some of your own visualisations in terms of how you (uniquely you) want your life to be...what you want it to look like and feel like. Visualise and affirm the positive.

Every time your ED starts to grab a hold of your thoughts, feelings or behaviours, remember what you felt like during this meditation, remind yourself of how you want to feel and affirm to yourself the qualities that you wish to embody.

What we would like to get you to eventually, is letting go of the obsession of weighing yourself, all together. This will take courage and grit, moving forward, but eventually, a healthy, happy, and harmonious life is what you will end up with. I am on this journey with you, and this is the next step, of letting go of your eating disorder entirely. Once we have found a bit more balance in our lives, by practicing a) throwing away your constant thoughts about weight – tearing up that piece of paper every day, and b) doing 10 minutes of balancing meditation/visualisation every day... this is the next step, to get rid of daily weighing, minimising the weighing, and god dammit... even throwing away those scales altogether!! Remember, we are on this epic journey together, dear reader.

Again, tell your eating disorder to F*** Off!

# A note for loved ones

The most important message that I would like to get across to family, friends and loved ones is that your loved one who is experiencing an eating disorder is separate from their ED. The ED may cause them to act in ways that are not aligned with who they truly are. The ED may get in the way of them living in alignment with their values and may get in the way of your unique relationship. The relationship may struggle, but this is only because their eating disorder changes who they are and affects the way they see themselves in their world. I would say to you.... Always encourage your loved one to remember who they truly are. Who they were, and who they may become. Encourage them to explore who they are, separate from their ED. Try and encourage them to dream about a life outside of their eating disorder, and encourage them to set goals – short-term and long-term. And help them to explore what is truly important to them (their values) and help them to explore different parts of their personality. Also.... Make them laugh and smile, anyway you can. This can be a nice reminder that your loved one is still in there, under the surface. Their sparkle has been dulled because of the disorder, so use your unique relationship to bring forth that sparkle, as often as you can.

    Try not to get too angry at them, or angry at the disorder, see things for what they are; be patient and kind. Remind your loved one that they are immeasurably strong and resilient, and that they can use their eating disorder traits in their own recovery journey. As I have outlined already in this book, the eating disorder traits can be flipped on their head and used for the positive. Determination, perseverance and even perfectionism, can be leveraged and used for their recovery from their ED. Remind your loved one to always have hope in recovery, never stop believing in recovery. And if your loved one is in the thick of illness and can't see a way forward, then hold the hope for them at all times; do not give up on them. This hope can and will rub off, as it did with me when I was at Hollywood Clinic. Encourage them to step out of their comfort zone and seek professional help from a dietician and/or a psychologist. Encourage them to challenge their eating disorder whenever they can. Small steps forward are still steps forward. Even if that means eating one snack more than they did yesterday, or skipping the scales for one day...see this as an act of courage... remind your loved one that it is possible to tell your eating disorder to F*** off... and remind them that this will make them feel empowered and good, even if it is scary at first. Once your loved one gets a taste for this kind of empowerment, they will be stronger for it and have more motivation to kick the ED to the kerb once and for all. And do not neglect your own needs, try and model good self-care and self-love. You cannot give from an empty cup, so remember to fill your cup consistently, so you can be there for your loved ones when they need your support and your strength.

Help your loved one to see that they are very much deserving of a happy, healthy life. They may question their self-worth at times but simply remind them that they deserve all the good things that life has to offer and encourage them to see this as an extremely likely possibility. Make plans with your loved one. If they like a certain place or location (or if they used to), go there with them, bring out that sparkle in their soul. Focus on bringing out their unique being every day, try not to focus on the ED too much, because any reminder of who they are at their core is going to silence the ED – even for a mere moment – and this is priceless. Try and model positive behaviour around food and exercise, make sure you nourish your body and show your loved ones the importance of doing so. Try and stay away from the scales, because this is something that your loved one will have to master at some point. Scales aren't healthy, they can turn into an obsession, which just feeds the eating disorder. I would also say, talk with your loved one about the concept of getting them back in the driver's seat of their own life and existence, as they need to know that this is a real possibility, once they are on the road to recovery. Any of these kinds of conversations will plant a seed in your loved one's psyche, which will come to fruition eventually. Trust that. Tell your loved one that they are beautiful inside and out, remind them that thinness is not the goal here, health and happiness are the goals.

And one last thing, try not to look at the 'why' of the eating disorder, and do not blame yourself or anyone else. Simply look forward; this is key.

# CHAPTER 6
# MANIFESTATION WORKBOOK

## • Introduction to manifestation

Now that you are starting to address your eating disorder issues, and you are telling your eating disorder to stick it! - You know who *you* are and what *you* want and value in life... this is the next step. Let's start building and creating the life that you now know *you* desire and 100 % *deserve*. This part of the process truly is the best, particularly if you are starting with a clean slate – this process can be incredibly exciting and empowering. If you are not starting with a clean slate, this process will absolutely still take you very much in the right direction, moving forward – towards a life that you love and cherish.

    The way that we are going to start building and creating this new, happy, healthy and fulfilling life is through the art of manifestation – I wish I knew about this when I started my recovery many moons ago!

    What is manifestation you might ask?

    Manifestation is the process of bringing forth events and experiences into your life through the energy you put out into the world. It is a term that describes the result of the Law of Attraction, a universal law where energy attracts like energy.

    Each and every one of us is manifesting all the time, but when we actively put our energy towards the life we want to live, that's when we can consciously create and manifest our dreams and desires.

I have put time and energy into my manifestation practice a lot over the past 5 years, by doing the exercises outlined below and an almost daily meditation practice - and I have attracted almost all of what I was desiring all the way back when. This included a loving partner, amazing friendships, wonderful jobs and other opportunities, a house to call our own and holidays – to name a few! In this chapter you will start to familiarize yourself with the concept, and really, you will have the opportunity to start your own practice – and attract your hearts desires.

I think that this is the perfect time to do so, as your eating disorder may have led you towards a life you are not necessarily very happy with. But with that out the way.... (its ok if this is still a work in progress), you are free to create any sort of life that you want! – keeping your identified goals and values in mind.

The following exercises in this chapter will start you on your way, and I will be explaining them as we go along. Just remember, that with manifestation – mindset is everything! So, to keep your spirits high and to keep you feeling inspired, there are some quotes about manifestation below! I find that seeing these sorts of quotes consistently is an uplifting reminder of where I am heading, and they help me to stay in a positive mindset about manifesting my desires. You can also make manifestation quotes a part of your daily ritual, using them in a similar way to affirmations and mantras to get in the right mindset to manifest.

So, here are some powerful quotes about manifestation:

"The Law of Attraction states that whatever you focus on, think about, read about, and talk about intensely, you're going to attract more of into your life."
Jack Canfield

"I attract into my life whatever I give my attention, energy, and focus to, whether positive or negative."
Michael Losier

"See yourself living in abundance and you will attract it."
Rhonda Byrne

"Imagination is everything. It is the preview of life's coming attractions."
Albert Einstein

"When you visualize, then you materialize. If you've been there in the mind, you'll go there in the body."
Dr. Dennis Waitley

"When you are truly clear about what you want, the whole universe stands on tiptoe waiting to assist you in miraculous and amazing ways to manifest your dream or intention."
Constance Arnold

"To bring anything into your life, imagine that it's already there."
Richard Bach

"Eliminate all doubt and replace it with the full expectation that you will receive what you are asking for."
Rhonda Byrne

So, now you are more familiar with manifestation and how powerful it can be, and now that you recognise that you deserve a wonderful, fulfilling, happy life... let the work begin!

## • Free writing exercise

Grab a pen and a timer. Set a timer for 10 minutes. Write a heartfelt letter to your present-day self from your future self, outlining all the wonderful things you have in your life. This future self could be you one year from now, five years from now or twenty-five years from now... whatever resonates with you.

The trick to free writing is to keep writing until the timer goes off. Don't pause, don't edit, don't judge and don't try to think too much. The beauty of this exercise is that it pulls stuff from your subconscious mind that might not necessarily come out if you were to take the time to stop and think about it. And THINK BIG! Nobody but you is going to read this.

# TELL YOUR EATING DISORDER TO F*** OFF

## See the life you want exercise

Close your eyes and picture your life as it will be when you have everything you desire to manifest.

- What does a day in your life look like?
- How does your day unfold?
- Who is there?
- What do you eat?
- How do you play?
- How does it feel to witness yourself in these states?

Feel free to get detailed with your visualisations. The more clearly you can see these things, the more you will believe they are possible. Write any notes for anything that comes up, so you can easily refer back to this.

# TELL YOUR EATING DISORDER TO F*** OFF

## Setting intentions

**What are intentions?**

When attempting manifestation, it's important that you're clear on what you want to start creating in your life. That's why a well-rounded manifestation practice starts out with clear intentions.

An intention is different to a goal or wish. An intention is something you practice in each and every moment. It's about enjoying the journey as much as the destination. It doesn't have a specific timeframe, checklist or pass/fail conclusion. It's mindful, fluid and open to change, and built on values and feelings. Think of an intention as a way to direct your energy.

**Four Pointers**

1. Try not to set more than 5 intentions at a time. If we have too many intentions, they begin to lose their power.

2. Language is key with the 3 Ps:

   - **PRESENT** – intentions are most powerful when we write them in the present tense. Good intention starters are 'I am', 'I have', or 'I feel'
   - **POSITIVE** – Keep it positive. Rather than writing 'I no longer have toxic relationships in my life', write 'I am in a loving, respectful and joyful relationship'.
   - **POTENT** – Keep them short and sharp. Get to the point in one or two sentences – any longer and the intention loses its potency.

3. Don't worry about the specifics. As soon as we try to answer the how, when, where and why, we start to set parameters for our intention, and we narrow the ways in which it can manifest.

4. You can't set an intention for someone else.

Using your free writing exercise as a guide, extract five intentions that you want to work with.

# TELL YOUR EATING DISORDER TO F*** OFF

Now attach one feeling to each of your intentions. How would having that manifest make you feel?

Once each intention is vibrationally charged with feeling, your job is to feel into those feelings as often as possible.

This part is non-negotiable. If you can't connect with the feeling of already having your intention, then you will find it hard to attract that intention towards you.

## • Action steps

Grab a pen and your five intentions (which now have feelings behind them). For each intention, write down one action step that you can take today to move yourself one step closer.

If the idea of taking action feels overwhelming, go smaller. Even start with something as simple as I will start believing that I am worthy and capable of manifesting my intentions.

Each week address new action steps that you can take for your intention. Some weeks these steps will be big and bold, and some weeks they won't. That's ok!

| INTENTION: | ACTION STEP: |
|---|---|
|  |  |
|  |  |
|  |  |
|  |  |
|  |  |
|  |  |

## • Life domains

Looking at life domains is a good way to see what concrete action you can take to follow your path. Here is a list of domains that could be a good starting point:

| | | |
|---|---|---|
| Career or work | Legacy | Sleep/rest |
| Community involvement | Leisure | Spirituality/religion |
| Creativity | Living environment | Travel |
| Family | Passions | Volunteering |
| Finances | Personal Presentation | Habits |
| Pets and Animals | Health and Fitness | Relationships/friendships |
| Holidays | Routine | Interests |
| Self-care | Learning and study | Service |

Choose the life domains that are relevant to you. Record them in the first column of the chart below and then record the actions you could take:

| LIFE DOMAIN | ACTIONS TO TAKE |
|---|---|
| | |
| | |
| | |
| | |
| | |
| | |

## Dream Job Visualisation

When I first started doing this exercise, I would get bogged down in the logistics of this dream job. Big mistake! A reminder: specifics just fence us in. So don't worry about your current skill set, don't focus on corporate ladders and don't get too concerned if the exact role that you want doesn't currently exist. Just dream big!

If you could do anything or be anything in your career, what would that be? Write it down in one of the following ways.

- Write a job description for your dream role and your dream company.
- Write a summary of your dream business.

This exercise gives you something to aim for. Even if it feels unachievable right now, you're cracking open a window to let a little possibility, hope and potential in!

## • The Tree of Love Exercise

Grab some colourful pens or pencils and a large piece of paper (like butcher's paper).

**STEP 1:** Draw the outline of a large tree. It must include roots, a thick trunk, and branches.

**STEP 2:** The roots of your tree represent your new beliefs about love. Write them as positive and present intentions. For example, I am love. I am at peace with love. I trust in commitment and connection. Love is abundant in my life.

**STEP 3**: The trunk of the tree represents the feelings you want to vibrate in relationships. These might be peace, freedom, abundance, security, stability and excitement.

**STEP 4:** The branches of the tree are the actions that support your intentions. Write your action steps along the branches. For example, I open my eyes and my heart to new possibilities. I smile and make eye contact with strangers. I receive compliments from people without deflecting them. I show up for love, I radiate love out into the world.

**STEP 5:** Finally, add some leaves to your tree. These are your love adornments. They are things that make you feel the high vibrations of love – activities you absolutely love doing, such as writing, practicing yoga, spending time with a pet, reading in bed on a Sunday morning, volunteering, meditating.

Place your Tree of Love somewhere that you will see it every day, as a reminder to tap into the vibrations of love and take action steps in the direction of love.

## Peaceful Breathing For Intuitive Guidance

- Bring your awareness to a problem in need of a solution
- Close your eyes and tune into your natural breath
- Place both hands gently over your belly. Notice the inhale, the pause at the top, the exhale and the pause at the bottom
- Slowly begin to deepen the breath, feeling the subtle sensation of your hands rising and falling with each inhale and each exhale
- Tap into the feeling of peace. With each inhale and exhale breath, feel peace slowly flood through every cell of your body. Stay here for as long as you need
- Once peace has become your vibration (and it will if you keep breathing), then you'll have a clear channel to your inner guidance

**Intuitively, what do you believe is the next step forward? Without asking for confirmation from someone else, and without googling it or taking a poll on your Instagram stories, can you have faith in your own choices and faith that you are being supported by the universe?**

## Self-love in practice

**Self Love Inspection**

**Answer the following questions (and be honest with yourself):**

1. What are the five things preventing you from loving yourself completely?
2. If you could change any five things about yourself, inside or out, what would they be? And why?
3. If you were told that none of these things you've listed in the previous two questions could be changed, could you love yourself despite them?

## Self-Love Energy Suckers

Let's start by dividing your life into four main areas.

1. Physical appearance
2. Relationships
3. Career
4. Finances

In terms of self-love, self-worth, and self-esteem, where are you wasting your energy in these areas of your life? Ask yourself what counterproductive thoughts, feelings and actions are preventing you from having higher vibrations in these areas?

## Positive Self-Love

Start by answering this question: how do you want to feel about yourself?

Let's get more specific. Go through the same four main areas we divided your life into in the previous exercise when you were identifying where you were wasting your energy.

1. Physical appearance
2. Relationships
3. Career
4. Finances

Now that you've identified where you were wasting energy in each of those areas, replace that wasted energy with positive energy. How do you desire to feel in each of the areas listed above?

Can you feel each of those feelings right now in this moment without physically changing a single thing about yourself?

If you feel resistance behind this exercise, try and drop the negative stories around each area of your life. For example, if you want to feel happiness, joy and pride around your appearance, stop the internal voice from saying 'But I don't feel these things', or 'I'll feel those things when I'm this dress size or that weight'. Just feel the feelings separate from the story, right now in this very moment.

## • Kate's Daily Manifestation Meditation Practice'

I am going to walk you through my daily meditation practice and suggest that you replicate this as much as possible. Of course, yours will differ from mine somewhat, as what you are wanting to manifest may be very different from my own desires.

Essentially, I believe that without my meditation practice, there would be very little manifestation. My meditations have been tailored by me to include all the practices that are vital if you're wanting to nail manifestation.

This includes affirmations, visualisations and what I refer to as "feeling into" whatever it is that you deeply desire. I practice this daily for about 30 minutes, and that is truly all the time that it requires.

Let us begin.

I start off by repeating this prayer, which I have taken from Gabrielle Bernstein's 'The Universe has Your Back'.

"Today I surrender my goals and plans to the care of the Universe. I offer up my agenda and accept spiritual guidance. I trust that there is a plan far greater than mine. I know that where there once was lack and limitation there are spiritual solutions and creative ideas. I step back and let love lead the way. Thy will be done".

This lets the universe know that I mean business.

 I then continue by repeating this mantra: "I deeply surrender my goals, plans and agenda to the universe today, I accept spiritual guidance, and I know I am supported every step of the way."

I take a few deep breaths and let go.

 I continue by repeating the following statement "I deeply surrender my worries and concerns to the care of the universe".

At the same time when repeating this, I visualise and feel into each of my worries/concerns and consciously let the worry go. I immediately feel lighter.

 I then go through all the main domains of my life, and surrender each part of my life, to the love and wisdom of the universe.

For instance: "I deeply surrender my employment situation to the care of the universe".

I feel into what I want I want to be experiencing in this domain, such as feeling accomplished and abundant, and I visualise myself doing the job that I desire.

 Then I move onto other life domains, such as financial situation, love-life situation and living situation.

Again, this will differ according to what you're wanting to manifest and attract into your life.

Then I move onto "I allow myself to release any attachment to these outcomes"

This tells the universe that I don't need these manifestations to materialize before I am actually happy or joyful…I will feel happy, joyful and abundant anyway…. and hence be in an emotional state that will attract more good things.

We cannot wait for the perfect job, the perfect romantic partner or perfect apartment before we are happy. It is imperative that we feel good, even if we don't have these things. The universe works faster when you're feeling positive and grateful, and when you are having fun!! So, it is your job to ramp up these positive feelings as much as you can every day, if you want to nail manifestation.

 I then go on to repeat the following: "I feel free to live in the moment, with peace, love, joy, immense gratitude and abundance".

I feel into these emotions as I repeat them. I do this about 3 times.

 This follows with "I am open to infinite possibilities, spiritual solutions, and creative opportunities".

We must be open to all creative solutions because the universe often works in miraculous, mysterious ways.

 I then move onto "I am a magnet for miracles"

And then visualise and feel into each outcome that I want to manifest, whether that be good health, better finances, a specific employment outcome, or a more exciting and fulfilling romantic life. I repeat this at least 2 times.

 Then I repeat "I have deep faith in the universe's plan",

And again, I visualise and feel into the outcomes that I want. I repeat this twice and end by repeating the same mantra, but then completely letting go of how the manifestations will materialise. I breathe deeply and feel into feelings of complete faith.

- Then I repeat one of my favourite affirmations: "I am happy and whole",

  And I repeat this several times, breathing in wholeness and positivity.

- Also "I am healthy, balanced and aligned", to initiate feelings of total balance.

  A feeling of calm and joy should accompany this mantra.

- I then move on to repeating "I am happy and excited".

  I repeat this whilst going through a set of visualisations. Things that make me feel excited and happy, and I feel into each of these also. For instance, I visualise and feel into living in the perfect house, with my romantic partner by my side; I visualise and feel into entertaining guests in my lovely house, and I visualise and feel into going on a road trip holiday with my romantic partner. Whatever you wish to visualise and feel into in this step, is completely up to you depending on what it is that you want to manifest. I generally go through about 8-10 different manifestations in this step. But even a few things is fine.

- I then move onto repeating, "I am happy and secure"

  Because this is something I have always yearned for. I visualise and feel into my romantic partner holding me tightly and visualise a happy engagement and marriage. Again, you work with whatever it is that you specifically want to manifest, and this could be something completely different to my deepest desires.

- I then move onto even more of a focus on my romantic life. I repeat "I am loved and supported every step of the way".

  I visualise and feel into different parts of what this manifestation could look like. I visualise and feel into holding hands with my romantic partner and see us walking hand in hand near a lake. I visualise and feel into cuddling on our couch or receiving a bunch of flowers. Get creative with this step and have a think about exactly what you would like to experience here.

Moving on, I repeat, "I am proud", "I am accomplished, and "I am abundant". Visualise and feel into each of these statements, according to what each of these statement means for you. For instance, I visualise and feel into having my second book published or feeling proud to walk hand-in-hand with my romantic partner.

When I repeat "I am abundant", I simply feel into feelings of overflowing abundance. This should feel really nice.

I end my meditation by going back to the mantra "I have deep faith in the universe's plan."

And I simply feel into the sense of complete and total faith in the universe. Again, this should feel like a letting go of sorts.

---

Note:

I have been able to manifest almost everything I have wanted in the past 5 years, since I began this practice. I manifested a house, a loving partner, a great job, great friends, a publisher for my books, and many other joys in my life to this day. The only thing I had left to work on really, was getting this eating disorder out of the way of my happiness and wellbeing...and I am well on this path now!

So, Happy manifesting angels!

# CONCLUSION

What can I possibly say to round off this incredible journey that we have been on together? It's been epic, reflecting on all the things that make me want to move forward in my life without an eating disorder as a part of that. I started writing this book in July 2024 and it is now December 2025. And I have come so far. More recently, as I have said already, my weight was dropping – a few months ago. But I have come so far in the past few months, and made so much headway, that I feel it is necessary to finish writing this self-help book. I still have a little way to go, just this morning I stepped onto the scales (weekly now, not daily), and I struggled with the number. But I am much less focused on being thin, and much less focused on that number staring back at me. I have a new goal in the next couple of weeks, to cut back to monthly weighing. And who knows from there, I may get rid of the scales altogether! You do the same, dear reader... take *your power* back.

The scales make me stressed and unhappy. And for what? What is its purpose? Sure, I will keep tabs on it because of my unique situation with anti-psychotic medication. But I would like to get to the point where I can simply go by clothing – rather than seeing a number to obsess about endlessly.

One of the greatest learnings I have experienced – only over the last couple of months – is that our bodies need nourishment. A lot of it. And that is more than OK. Our bodies are our only vehicle in this journey through life, and we must take care of it. At the end of the day, appearance shouldn't be the focus. Health should be the focus. Sure, it is still OK to take pride in yourself and wear nice clothing to express yourself and even do your make-up – this is just good self-care. But weight? Not an issue. Not one that matters anyway. I have learnt, aside from this lesson around nourishment, that food is not the enemy. Every meal and snack that we eat is an opportunity to show self-love through nourishment. Food is medicine. Remember that. It is OK to enjoy food, and I know that enjoying food with the people I love in this life is one of life's greatest joys. Do not deny yourself of that, do not deny that little girl/boy inside that deserves love and happiness. Make plans with the people you love to enjoy food, because this helps you be accountable – and helps keep you motivated to kick your ED's arse.

We are lovable – regardless of our size. Size 8, 12, 16, 20.... It doesn't matter; we are lovable regardless. If by chance you are struggling with not having enough support from others, then push your comfort zone to meet new people and find your tribe. This life is not meant to be lived in isolation. Let that be your goal – to find other people who are on this journey called life and enjoy life with them – have fun and seek out pleasure. This tells your eating disorder to F*** right off.

Laugh out loud. Enjoy life. As I have said previously, this is like kryptonite to your ED. It cannot survive in the light of your true sparkly soul. Remember that. When your eating disorder gets louder – which it will – whilst on this recovery path, remember how strong and resilient you are. Put up a fight, don't give in to its soul-crushing, punishing ways. Don't let your eating disorder dull that beautiful sparkle of yours. Remember your sparkle and remember what keeps that sparkle alive. Do that. Constantly. Remember what is actually important to you and remember who you are – without your ED. What do *you* want in *your* future? What do *you* see? When you get to the end of your one precious life, you will feel proud that you kicked your ED's butt... you will feel proud that you fought the battle and won. You will win, dear reader, just remember why you're doing this, remember why you're putting up a fight. An eating disorder is indeed a disgusting thing – even when we explore the fact that it can be an ally – and is trying to keep you safe – remember that at its core, it is making you unhappy – and sick. Don't waste your precious time obsessing over weight. It is absolutely pointless.

I feel that if you keep all of this in mind, moving forward, you are going to kick your ED to the kerb – you are in the process of telling it to F*** right off. This journey is extremely challenging, but how good will you feel at the end of it? An epic win on the eating disorder front will lead to an epic life moving forward. Your resilience, your courage, your innate sense of hope, will lead you towards happiness and a life that you love. The results will be like night and day in comparison. You will be so grateful for this journey – you will be grateful for the little things *and* the big things, and life will never be the same again. Think of this journey you're on as character building and think of it as a reminder to be happy and grateful every day, moving forward.

    I am so proud of you, dear reader, for going on this journey with me. You are amazing for just the fact that you picked up this book and allowed yourself to even consider fighting this epic battle. The work that you have been doing since you picked up this book is amazing, and I truly hope you have changed your perspective. I truly hope you have found a bit of excitement and anticipation when considering how amazing your life will be when you get rid of this thing once and for all. Keep exploring who you are, keep finding ways to express yourself, and keep finding ways to prioritise your happiness and wellbeing. The excitement I felt when I first started battling anorexia was incredible, as prior to that, I truly believed that I was destined to live under the control of my eating disorder forever. So, other than continuing to explore who you truly are, also explore what you want in life. Because the sky is the limit. Use the manifestation tools that I have included in this book, to manifest to your heart's desire! Your life can be anything you want it to be! Your life can be anything you dream it to be! I truly believe this, dear reader, and let the fact that you have lived under the control of an eating disorder for however long.... be the reason you will make the rest of your life, the best of your life!

    Good luck, you amazing human beings.
    You've got this. Enjoy the journey.
    Let your soul sparkle.
    And remember.... Tell Your Eating Disorder to F**k Off!!!
    Love Kate xxxx

# ACKNOWLEDGEMENTS

Leon: I want to acknowledge you, Leon, for supporting me and being a bright, shiny, happy (and carefree) light in my life even when I experience darkness. You may not understand what I am going through with my ED issues, but whenever I am talking to you, or whenever we are just together, I forget all that stuff. Our very special relationship helps me to remember who I am and to remember what is important in life. PS Thank you for hiding the bathroom scales even when you thought I would bite your head off for doing so hahaha.

Mum: I want to acknowledge you, mum, at this time, because despite the fact you went on a tumultuous journey with me and my anorexia in my teenage years, you are still able to support me with stuff that I know that you thought was gone for good. Alas, an ED reared its ugly head again however, I know I can always count on you to listen to me non-judgementally. Thank you for just being amazing, I don't know what I would do without you.

Bev: Bev, you are someone I can trust to talk to about this stuff, and there is never any judgment coming from you at all. You are brutally honest, which I definitely need sometimes, and you invite humour into the equation, which is so valuable. And we still catch up and have fun! Which puts the ED right back in its box. Also... Thank you for putting me on the right path to find an amazing psychologist when things began to go downhill a little bit. I am so grateful for this, and I am so grateful for your friendship and amazing support.

Tara: As someone who truly understands this stuff, Tara. Your friendship and support are invaluable to me. You have made it clear to me recently that you are there for me to support me when I need it most, and that means so much to me. You are one of the most beautiful and intelligent people I know, and you always bring your amazing words of wisdom to our delightful conversations! And also, thank you for helping me find the right support with my wonderful dietician. I honestly wouldn't have kicked this thing as I have in recent times, without the support of a dietician who truly gets it and helped me to tell my eating disorder to get stuffed. I am so grateful that I know you and can call you my dear friend.

www.ingramcontent.com/pod-product-compliance
Lightning Source LLC
Chambersburg PA
CBHW020110240426
43661CB00002B/95